COMPANION WORKBOOK TO
LIFE IN ITS RAWEST FORM

Companion Workbook To

LIFE IN ITS RAWEST FORM

A True Story of Perseverance and Triumph

QIANA HICKS

Copyright ©2017 by Qiana Hicks

Published by Words of Inspiration Publishing, LLC
First Edition

All rights reserved. No part of this book may be reproduced, scanned, or distributed in any printed or electronic form without authorized approved written permission of author and publisher except in the case of brief quotations embodied in critical reviews and certain other noncommercial uses permitted by copyright law. For permission requests, contact the publisher, with the subject addressed "Attention: Permissions Coordinator," at the email address: wordsofinspirationpublishing@gmail.com

Neither the publisher nor the author is engaged in rendering professional advice or service to the individual reader. The ideas, suggestions, and procedures contained in this book are not intended as a substitute for consulting with your own personal professional support system.

Copyediting by Natalie M. Rotunda
rotunda56303@hotmail.com • (320) 203-7433

Edited by Mary Beth Ruhland • Editor and Publications Specialist • Eagan, MN
mbruhland@gmail.com • (651) 470-9519

Visit the author website: www.qianahicks.com
Contact Information: wordsofinspirationpublishing@gmail.com

Words of Inspiration
PUBLISHING

ISBN 978-0-9986180-3-6 (Paperback Cover)

BIO023000 BIOGRAPHY & AUTOBIOGRAPHY/African American & Blacks
SEL021000 SELF-HELP/Motivational & Inspirational

CONTENTS

INTRODUCTION 7

ONE: Families Battling Addiction 9
    1.1 Different Methods For Getting Help Or Change 12
    1.2 Recovery And Support 22

TWO: Families In Transition 27
    2.1 The Effects Of Transition 28
    2.2 Controlling Your Emotions While In Transition 31
    2.3 Utilizing The Resources Around You To Help With Your Transition ... 34

THREE: Teenage Pregnancy 39
    3.1 Preventive Measures 41
    3.2 Abstinence, Celibacy, And Contraceptives 44
    3.3 Using Time Constructively 52
    3.4 Adolescent Parenting 54
    3.5 Making Adjustments—Doing Things Differently 58
    3.6 Two Teenaged Parents Are Better Than One 60
    3.7 Breaking The Cycle 63
    3.8 Being Accountable And Taking Responsibility As A Teenage Parent ... 66
    3.9 Making Lifestyle Changes To Become A Better Me For My Child 69
    3.10 Break The Cycle—Choose To Be Different 72

FOUR: Setting Goals And Executing Them 77
    4.1 Making Plans For Your Future 78
    4.2 Changes For The Better 84
    4.3 Getting Through Obstacles And Roadblocks 87

FIVE: Choosing The Right Role Model For You 89
    5.1 Identifying The Right Role Model For Me 90
    5.2 Helping You Help Me 94
    5.3 Chose Your Role Model Wisely 96
    5.4 Where To Find The Right Role Model For You 97
    5.5 You Can Be A Role Model, Too 97

SIX: Leaving The Past In The Past 103
    6.1 Suffering May Occur In Many Forms 103
    6.2 Learning To Cope With Your Past 107

SEVEN: Managing Your Emotions Effectively 111
    7.1 Identify What Is Causing You To Become Emotional 113
    7.2 Acknowledge The Reality Of The Situation 115

APPENDIX 121
    A 121
    B 125
    C 131
    D 139
    E 145
    F 153
    G 159

INTRODUCTION

The purpose of this *Workbook* is to provide readers with an interactive version of *Life In Its Rawest Form*. It contains exercises and tools for effective self-empowerment, which you can reference and use regularly.

I've included topics from my book that helped me—and that I hope will help you—to become a better person. I've included information that *could have* made a positive difference in the adversities I experienced as both a child and youth. I've shared experiences here that led to successful outcomes, and those that did not lead to successful outcomes.

My goal in providing this *Workbook* is to help anyone who lives in similar circumstances to make informed decisions that will lead to a better outcome. My goal is to empower you, no matter what your background, to overcome your past by not allowing it to define your future. Throughout the *Workbook*, I share ideas that helped me overcome my past challenges and move forward into a bright, positive future.

The information I share in all seven chapters of this *Workbook* has played a significant role in the person I am today. It helped me break through obstacles and face challenges that led to better decisions, while helping me live with my past – *the good and the not-so-good* experiences.

This *Workbook* laser-focuses on helping disadvantaged youth and at-risk youth overcome challenges you were born into, or those that are outside of your control.

I grew up in those situations, so I understand what that life is like. I was born into poverty. I was raised by a single mother who battled both alcohol and drug addictions. I was that youth whose father spent the first half of my life in prison. My stepfather was abusive and addicted to drugs and alcohol, and he was in and out of our lives. I lived in a community where resources and opportunities were scarce, where drug and alcohol addiction, violence, and low education rates were the norm.

This *Companion Workbook* to my book, *Life In Its Rawest Form,* can help **you** overcome similar adversity. Use it as a platform to seek help for yourself, or to seek help for others. Also, use it to provide constructive criticism and feedback on ways Family Services professionals and establishments can improve and enhance their support for families in crisis.

Read and use recommendations that can help your family get through its transition more effectively. Most of the focus is on improving services for children and youth who are displaced from their homes to help them cope during their transition.

The *Workbook* also addresses common issues found in impoverished communities and adolescent parenthood. Topics relate to *disadvantaged youth, at-risk youth, teen pregnancy, drug and alcohol addictions, abuse, low education success rates*, and more.

I've included methods I've found to be effective in defeating the odds by using misfortunes to create a brighter future for yourself and your loved ones. Methods include:

- Teen pregnancy prevention
- Breaking the cycle
- Managing emotions
- Setting goals
- Selecting a role model
- Planning for a brighter future

Another purpose of the *Workbook* is to provide a way for you, whether you are a child, a youth, or an adult, to proactively seek opportunities that will make your life better and improve your circumstances.

I recommend that you use the information and activities to interact with people and resources who will help you to improve your situation.

I **strongly** recommend that you do not just write in the *Workbook*, then toss it aside. It's intended for you to use it regularly while working to improve your present and future. Use it to track your progress, and use it as a reference guide. Share it with others so they can understand how to best help you.

Use the *Workbook* for what it's worth—a working guide for you, a work-in-progress.

CHAPTER 1

FAMILIES BATTLING ADDICTION

Addictions, no matter what kind they are, can greatly oppress families and loved ones. Addiction is an illness. It causes people to do negative and harmful things they wouldn't do if they were not under the influence of drugs or alcohol.

While choosing to get high, most addicts do not take into consideration the trouble their choices cause their loved ones. Ironically, it's family members and loved ones who suffer more than the person with the addiction. They're usually left to pick up the pieces and repair the damages.

Ever since I can remember, my mother, father, and stepfather battled drug and alcohol addiction. It caused significant turmoil within our family and impacted me and my siblings. We survived, but we endured a great deal of trauma before our parents got professional help.

My brother and sister and I were eventually taken from our home. We lived apart, in separate places, while our parents either sought court-ordered professional help, or were incarcerated for unlawful actions committed while under the influence.

Living through such troubled times caused a great deal of adversity and oppression, due, directly and indirectly, to unfortunate situations where I was mentally or physically hurt. My siblings also suffered undue stress and physical and mental pain because of our parents' addictions. I tried and my siblings tried relentlessly to make our mother aware of how her actions were affecting us, but to no avail. Unfortunately, it wasn't enough to prevent harmful situations from taking place.

In this chapter, the main point is to discuss common issues and concerns that exist within families where one or both parents battle drug or alcohol addiction. How do their addictions affect you? Express your thoughts and feelings here, then share this information with them. Make them aware of how their behaviors affect you. Share with them your hopes—that they will change for the better.

In the exercise below, I ask you to share personal information and how it relates to drug and alcohol abuse and addiction. I realize this may be difficult for you. You may have been instructed by your parents or other family members not to share information with anyone outside of your home.

However, this exercise may help you and your loved ones get the help your parents need in order to help *you*. By completing this and other exercises, sharing information about your problems at home can actually **prevent** you and your loved ones from ongoing hurt because of your parents' illness.

It may even save your lives.

Are you or is anyone in your family suffering from drug or alcohol addiction? If yes, who? Put a ✓ in the appropriate box or boxes below:

	MOM	DAD	SELF	SIBLINGS	OTHERS
DRUG ADDICTION					
ALCOHOL ADDICTION					

If you put a ✓ in any of the boxes above, answer the following questions. If not, skip to the next section of the chapter.

Have you addressed the issue with your loved ones? If yes, how did you address it?

_____
_____
_____
_____

How did they respond or react?

_____
_____
_____
_____

Have you looked for help outside of your home? If yes, please explain.

_____
_____
_____
_____

Please note: Additional space to continue this exercise can be found in Appendix A.

SECTION 1.1

Different Methods For Getting Help Or Change

There are several tools and resources available to help people with drug and alcohol addiction, as well as for their family and loved ones. It's important to remember that we're all different, and every addiction affects people in different ways.

There are some people who, fortunately, have never had to experience drug or alcohol addiction themselves, or had to deal with loved ones who are addicted. They may not understand that quitting isn't always simple. *We*, who are affected in some way, understand it isn't simple. As often as we share with our parents or loved ones how their addiction affects us, most of the time it isn't reason enough to make them quit.

In rare cases, all it takes to quit is to be made aware of how their addiction hurts their children or loved ones. That doesn't mean their addiction is any less serious than those not able to quit for that reason. What it means is: ***What works for one person may not work for another***, *hence* the earlier statement that addiction affects people in different ways.

Be transparent and open with your parents about how their addiction affects you. It's one of the best ways to help them fight their addiction. The more your parents are aware of how their behavior hurts or impacts you or loved ones, the harder they'll fight to quit. While this method has been proven to be effective for some, it's not guaranteed to work for everyone. The idea is this: Hearing, firsthand, the danger or harm their addiction has caused the people they love can have a bearing on the level of effort they'll put into kicking their addiction. It's worth a try. Always be open with your parents, tell them specific things that hurt you, even if *they* are the source of the hurt. Their habits may not change immediately, but, someday, a light may go on in their heads that will allow them to listen and process what you tell them. Being informed can make a difference in one's decisions and actions.

Speak up, and don't be discouraged. Your voice may be just what your loved ones need to seek help.

In this exercise, use your voice to tell your parents or loved ones what you want them to hear. Tell each person you identified in the previous exercise just how his or her addiction(s) affects you. Hold nothing back. There are no limitations or restrictions on what you share. Don't be concerned about who will see this information, and don't fear what will happen. When you've finished, if you decide against sharing this information with your parents or loved ones, use it to seek professional help, or help from someone you trust.

Describe how you feel about your parents' drug and/or alcohol addiction(s).

_____
_____
_____
_____
_____
_____
_____
_____
_____
_____
_____
_____
_____

Tell your parents or loved ones how their addictions and behaviors have affected you. This may include but may not be limited to:

- Watching how your siblings are also being hurt by their actions
- School
- Work
- Health (physical, mental, strength, etc.)
- Relationships
- Mood

Please note: *Additional space to continue this exercise can be found in Appendix A.*

In the table below, identify (✓) everyone who is impacted by their addictions and substance abuse:

	MOM	DAD	SELF	SIBLINGS	OTHERS
DRUG ADDICTION					
ALCOHOL ADDICTION					

How has your day-to-day life changed due to your parents' addiction or substance abuse issues?

_____
_____
_____
_____
_____
_____
_____
_____
_____

How can their fight to overcome their addiction change your life?

_____
_____
_____
_____
_____
_____
_____
_____
_____
_____

Please note: *Additional space to continue this exercise can be found in Appendix A.*

Recognizing that a person has an addiction is half the battle. Becoming aware of how that addiction affects loved ones or others is another critical component in getting help.

Drug and alcohol addiction is an illness that affects you and everyone else who is close to the user. The user is not the only one in need of help; **you** need help as well. An addict's loved ones tend to suffer significant adversity, due to the negative outcome of the substance abuse. Most addicts are not aware of the problems their choices cause you and others until after the fact.

You and your family members need to be educated on how to cope with parents or loved ones who have an addiction to drug and/or alcohol. You need help to understand that **you** are *not* responsible for their actions.

You should also learn how to **not allow** their behaviors to affect your health and well-being. It's not easy, but it is extremely important to learn these coping skills. If you do not learn them, you could spend much of your life being negatively affected by their addiction and behaviors. I know, firsthand, what this is like, and I wouldn't wish it on my worst enemy.

While I was growing up, my parents battled alcohol and drug addiction *simultaneously*. That quadrupled the issues going on in our household. Their addictions were the root cause for most of the trauma my siblings and I experienced—and those traumas spilled over into our adult lives, which were affected in many unhealthy ways.

For instance, we were damaged mentally, emotionally, psychologically, and physically. I wish we had had the opportunity to find and use resources to help us cope with the unhealthy and harmful situations. Unfortunately, we weren't so lucky. We endured quite a bit of trauma before any help came.

In addition to sharing how their addiction affects you in the exercises above, seek help from any of these eight resources:

- A school employee or faculty member
- Your teacher
- Your Pastor or someone at church
- A neighbor or a friend
- A Family Services professional
- Other family members
- Support groups
- The authorities

In this exercise, you'll describe the approach you would take to seek help, and what you hope to gain from that help. Use this as an actual opportunity to seek help from one of the resources listed above. Your response should sound as if you were speaking directly to them:

School employee or faculty member
(Principal, Administrative Staff, Nurse, Counselor, Advisor, etc.)

_____
_____
_____

Your teacher

_____
_____
_____

Your Pastor or someone at church

_____
_____
_____

A neighbor or a friend

_____
_____
_____

A Family Services professional

_____
_____
_____

Please note: *Additional space to continue this exercise can be found in Appendix A.*

Asking for help is a first step, but an all-important first step, to improving your circumstances. Your voice may be what it takes for your parents to get the help they need.

Please—don't look at this first step as if it's a betrayal. The fact is, you may be enabling them to continue their abuse and avoid the repercussions if you are aware of the harm their behavior is causing and you don't seek help.

Please be aware—things may not change immediately when you ask for help. It may take time for the process to begin, but at least you've taken the first step on the long road of redemption for you and your loved ones.

Now that you're prepared to ask for help, take the next step: **Define what you hope to gain from this process.** For me, when I was living through my parents' substance abuse—mainly my mother's—some of the things I hoped to gain from her getting help were:

- Her complete sobriety
- Her health (I loved it when she gained weight, because it meant she was no longer using)
- Her happiness
- Stability for my family and me
- A safer environment
- Family unity
- Financial security
- Trusting her again
- Knowing that we were her priority and that she loved us more than any stupid addiction
- Believing in her again

💡 In this exercise, define everything you hope to gain from your parents' recovery from their addiction(s).

1. _____

2. _____

3. _____

4. _____

5. _____

Change is possible if you have hope. That may seem far-fetched while you're going through the process of getting better, but never give up hope. Keep thinking about the life you will have, the life you've always wanted, when your parents become sober and clean. The effort you make now will make a difference in their decision to receive help. Always show them that you are not giving up on them. Let them know they are ***not allowed*** to give up, either. Hold them accountable for their recovery.

Do the best you can to not allow their condition to negatively affect you. Keep your hopes alive, every day.

Earlier in this section, remember how we talked about having to show tough love to parents or loved ones at times? We discussed how their choice to get high affects you, your siblings, and other family members in an unhealthy way. Substance addiction is a tough habit to fight. It causes significant, detrimental trauma to you and your loved ones. This type of trauma can have long-term, unhealthy effects—unless you prevent that from happening while coping with the circumstances.

Remember—***you*** are not responsible for ***their*** behaviors. Your FIRST priority is your own health and well-being.

In this exercise, we'll explore ways you can prevent your parents' or loved ones' addiction from impacting you in an unhealthy way. This does *not* mean you don't love them or support them. It *does* mean that you're trying to remain as healthy as possible, while coping with their illness.

While I was dealing with my mother's addictions—both drug and alcohol—I didn't look for ways to keep from being negatively impacted by her illness. I ended up suffering from her addictions, just as if I was the one with the addictions. It was mentally and physically stressful for me, and I experienced several unhealthy and harmful situations throughout my growing-up years.

You don't have to experience what I went through. It's not too late to proactively make changes. If I could go back in time, I would have done these things to prevent her drug and alcohol addictions from affecting me:

1. *I would try harder not to allow my mother's decision to get high affect me mentally or physically.*
2. *I would continue to tell my mother how her decisions to get high were affecting our lives.*
3. *I would talk to family members or other trusted adults to get help.*
4. *I would take advantage of family services or community groups that teach children and youth how to cope with parents with addictions.*
5. *I would hold my mother accountable for her actions and not stress myself out trying to make up for them.*
6. *I would seek professional help or arrange for an intervention.*
7. _____
8. _____
9. _____
10. _____

In this exercise, identify ways you can prevent your parents' or loved ones' addictions from affecting you in an unhealthy way. Similar to the exercise I filled in above, list several things that will help you:

1. _____
_____

2. _____
_____

3. _____
_____

4. _____
_____

5. _____
_____

6. _____
_____

7. _____
_____

8. _____
_____

9. _____
_____

10. _____
_____

Please note: *Additional space to continue this exercise can be found in Appendix A.*

The purpose for doing the exercises above is to help you while you think through actions you can take when going through this painful rollercoaster with your parents. They may or may not choose to seek help to kick their habit—but you should not have to suffer.

Remain healthy and strong so you can help your parents or loved ones. We can easily fall victim to this illness, because we get pulled into the problems caused by their addictions. We feel obligated or compelled to make up for their shortcomings, but we don't realize we're only hurting ourselves by losing ourselves in the process. Before you realize what is happening, your health deteriorates; your mood changes; your school, work, or livelihood is impacted; your personal relationships are affected; and so much more.

Use the information from this exercise to become aware of what events are taking place in your life, then proactively keep them from harming you. Never think that you're turning your back on your parents, or walking away from them. You're actually helping them by taking care of yourself. You may be surprised to know that, if they were sober, they would agree with your efforts to protect yourself, and they would want you to be healthy and unaffected by their decisions.

SECTION 1.2

Recovery And Support

Those who get high don't act as responsibly as they do when they're sober. Nor are they conscious of the burden their behavior places on their loved ones. Their only thought is to get high, no matter the cost. You have a better chance of getting through to them when they're sober. Just know your words may go out the window the moment they get their next high. This painful rollercoaster causes their loved ones endless suffering.

Even though there are programs and resources available to help substance abusers overcome their addictions, help, unfortunately, isn't always the solution or the cure they need. Every addict and every addiction is different from every other addict and addiction. What works for some may not work for others. Therefore, it's hard to tell what will help an addict overcome their addiction.

It's also hard to predict when the recovery will take ***effect***. For some, it will be sooner; for others, it will come later.

Overall, addiction is unpredictable and uncontrollable, which is why it is important to keep encouraging your parents and loved ones, so they can overcome it.

Support and encouragement can go a long way with substance abusers. It's true that specialized treatment programs and resources have, on occasion, proven to be effective. It's also true that it may only take support and encouragement from loved ones as a cure to their addictions.

When all else fails, simply speak from the heart. Share how their sobriety significantly impacts how well you function in your daily life. Tell them, encourage them—that they have what it takes to beat their addiction. Tell them that you have all the faith in the world that they will succeed in beating their addiction.

Growing up, I always made an effort to show my mother how much more I loved and appreciated her when she was clean and sober. I would do silly things to make her laugh. I'd help out more, or simply do my best not to shake things up. I never stopped believing and hoping that, one day, that would be *enough*.

In this section, tell your parents or loved ones who are battling addiction(s) how it makes you feel when they're ***not*** under the influence. In helping them overcome their addiction(s), tell them the things you enjoy about them when they're not high or intoxicated. Share your most memorable moments during their sober times. Tell them how much different your life would be if they overcame their addiction.

If you had the opportunity to share with your parents or loved ones how their sobriety or lack of drug use makes you feel, what would you say?

MOTHER

What does your mother's sobriety or lack of drug use mean to you?
_____
_____

How does it make you feel?
_____
_____

How does her sobriety or lack of drug use positively affect your life?
_____
_____

What would you like to share with your mother about her decision to choose you over her addiction?
_____
_____

What do you enjoy most about your mother when she is sober or not using drugs?
_____
_____

Explain to your mother how much she, and the choices she makes, matters to you.
_____
_____

FATHER

What does your father's sobriety or lack of drug use mean to you?
_____
_____

How does it make you feel?
_____
_____

How does his sobriety or lack of drug use positively affect your life?
_____
_____

What would you like to share with your father about his decision to choose you over his addiction?
_____
_____

What do you enjoy most about your father when he is sober or not using drugs?
_____
_____

Explain to your father how much he, and the choices he makes, matters to you.
_____
_____

Living with parents who battle drug and alcohol addiction(s) is a traumatizing experience for children or loved ones. Overcoming drug or alcohol addictions is unpredictable. It can be a short-term or a long-term experience. It all depends on the addict's ability and willpower to live life without the need to get high or intoxicated. Meanwhile, children and loved ones suffer the consequences.

There is no science on how to overcome addiction. Neither is there one single, guaranteed method for getting cured. What works for one person may not work for another. The best you can do as a loved one is to continue encouraging them to keep on fighting. In some cases, providing love and support has been more effective than any treatment program or service.

Always remember that ***you are not responsible*** for their actions. It is ***not*** your battle to fight. ***Do*** provide support to the extent that it does not cause you harm or distress.

The exercises you've completed in this chapter will provide you with opportunities to seek various types of help. What you've discovered in each exercise are ways to let your parents know how much their addictions affect you and the family. The exercises also allow you to share the ***good things*** you admire about them when they are not under the influence, along with the ***bad things***, the problems their addictions cause you. By working these exercises, you've taken important steps in the recovery process.

Remember: There ***Is*** help for you, your parents, and loved ones.

CHAPTER 2

FAMILIES IN TRANSITION

The purpose of this chapter is to make you aware of how transition will affect you and your family. We'll identify the ways Family Services professionals can help minimize the impact of the process. We'll also explore ways to effectively cope with the changes you'll experience.

As a child, I was raised primarily by a single mother who battled drug and alcohol addiction, I suffered child abuse, which included physical abuse. Due to my mother's addictions, my siblings and I were placed in harm's way on a number of occasions. As a result, we underwent several transition periods.

In my book, *Life In Its Rawest Form*, I talked about my experiences while transitioning, and how those experiences impacted my life. I described the emotional rollercoaster, the challenges of living in temporary placement facilities, and the type of help I <u>wished</u> I'd been given to manage my transitions positively.

Millions of families need to transition because of drug or alcohol addiction and abuse. Each addiction can cause its own turmoil. Some transitions are easier than others, while some are more challenging. I've experienced both.

In the upcoming sections, we'll discuss the impact transitioning can have on you and how you can effectively manage situations as you go through them.

We'll also discuss ways to make your experience positive, along with ways to avoid the negative.

We'll talk about how Family Services and temporary living facilities can help make your transition smoother and more positive. In the end, hopefully you'll have enough information to make your transition as painless as possible.

SECTION 2.1

The Effects Of Transition

Having to live apart from your family or the daily environment you have grown accustomed to can be a difficult adjustment, especially for children and youth. The transition can have a profound effect on how you react to the change, which may influence your behavior, emotions, vulnerability, and your overall ability to adjust. This is why it's important to get help and to have the right support during this time.

Something that resonates with me is the lack of personal support and attention from temporary living facilities and from Family Services professionals. When I was undergoing transition, there was minimal to no support to help me deal with the events occurring in my life. Had I received this type of support, I believe my experience during these times could have been better, or I could have had a more positive outcome.

I've listed below what you might expect in your transition process:

Advantages for Families in Transition
- You and your family are able to get help.
- The process may save your life or the lives of your family members.
- The process may prevent worse things from happening.
- You experience a safer and healthier living environment.
- You receive the basic necessities you may have lacked at home.
- The process provides security and stability.
- The process leads to recovery.
- The process encourages parents to do better and try harder.

Disadvantages for Families in Transition
- You have no control of the situation.
- You must follow other people's rules (good or bad).
- Your situation can change in the next moment.
- You and your loved ones are separated.
- You no longer have a family unit, nor familiar surroundings.
- For some, it can be a lonely and scary experience.
- Nothing is certain.
- It can be long-term.
- It can be more harmful than your previous situation.

Being separated from loved ones, especially your parents and siblings, is often a deeply emotional experience. Feelings of emptiness and loneliness may lead to vulnerability or other behavioral issues.

Many children and youth struggle to adjust to new surroundings when placed in temporary homes. As a result, they act out, mainly because of fear and uncertainty.

When I was in this position, I had no idea how long the transition period would last. I didn't know when I would be able to see my mother and siblings again. I didn't know where I would end up when it was all over. I was kept in the dark, for the most part, and that made each day even more challenging. I struggled with the thought of not being there to protect my little sister while she went through transition. Days spent in group homes and foster homes became stressful and painful. I also missed my mother intensely, and my brother. I felt like I was the one being punished for something I didn't do and had no control over.

Having someone to talk to could have eased the stress and frustration I felt some days. I had no one I could directly go to for advice or counseling. It also didn't help that these places were cold and desolate. They lacked the homey feeling I longed for and missed. I felt like I was in some kind of an institution.

In this exercise, we'll explore ways to deal with your emotions as you move through transition. We'll identify various tactics you can use to make the process a much smoother one.

First, describe your emotions as you go through the process. Next, to help you adjust more easily to the changes, we'll look for ways to cope with the circumstances. Last, we'll brainstorm ideas that will help make your stay in temporary facilities a more positive experience. I'll start off by listing my emotions through various transitions.

MY EMOTIONS AND FEELINGS DURING TRANSITION	
1.	I'm very sad.
2.	I'm afraid.
3.	I feel alone.
4.	I miss my family immensely.
5.	I'm frustrated that I can't have contact with them.
6.	I'm unsure of what lies ahead.
7.	I don't want to be here.
8.	I want to go home.
9.	
10.	

Describe below some of the emotions you may be experiencing while going through transition:

YOUR EMOTIONS AND FEELINGS DURING TRANSITION	
1.	
2.	
3.	
4.	
5.	
6.	
7.	
8.	
9.	
10.	

Please note: *Additional space to continue this exercise can be found in Appendix B.*

Being able to identify and describe your emotions and feelings will help you manage them more effectively. Use them to inform others, too, so they have a better understanding of how they can help you with the changes.

In the next part of this chapter, we'll focus on the best ways to manage the emotions you described above. We'll use that information to identify ways to cope effectively with each emotion for a positive outcome.

SECTION 2.2

Controlling Your Emotions While In Transition

Now that you've identified some of the emotions you're experiencing with your transition, the next step is to learn *how* to manage your emotions. Being aware of your emotions during this difficult time will help you manage them more effectively, so that you'll have a positive outcome, in most cases. (Refer to **Chapter 7: Managing Your Emotions Effectively**.)

When I was placed in temporary living facilities, I was frustrated some of that time. My frustration showed through my interaction with others. On these days, I would become confrontational and combative, all because I missed my mother and family. Had I taken the time to reflect on my feelings and the events that were taking place, the trouble I caused myself could have been prevented.

The goal for this next exercise is to identify your emotions early on so that you prevent further damage to yourself and your situation.

In the spaces below, describe ways you can prevent your emotions from negatively impacting your behavior. I'll start off by using the emotions I described in a previous exercise.

EXAMPLE:

	EMOTION	PREVENTIVE MEASURE
1.	I'm sad.	Think positive thoughts: When I would see my family next. This transition is only temporary.
2.	I'm afraid.	Talk to someone – a counselor, my social worker, or a trusted adult. Let them know my fears.
3.	I feel alone.	Write letters to my loved ones. Surround myself with others. Participate in fun activities.
4.	I miss my family.	Ask to make a phone call to my family. Write them letters. Look at their pictures.
5.	I'm frustrated.	Find ways to turn frustration into positive energy. Participate in activities. Talk with someone, such as a counselor or trusted adult.
6.	I'm unsure about the future.	Ask my caseworker questions about my situation. Make sure I seek clarity about my situation.
7.	I don't want to be here.	Look for ways to make the best of my stay. Keep a positive attitude. Remember that this is only temporary.
8.	I want to go home.	Look forward to going home. Spend less time thinking about how long it will take.
9.		
10.		

Now it's your turn. Define specific ways you can manage your emotions effectively to avoid negative outcomes during your transition.

	EMOTION	PREVENTIVE MEASURE
1.		
2.		
3.		
4.		
5.		
6.		
7.		
8.		
9.		
10.		

Please note: Additional space to continue this exercise can be found in Appendix B.

By doing these exercises, you're proactively and constructively looking for ways to manage your feelings to avoid making matters worse. Often, when families go through transition, the impact on children or youth can be negative and cause a rocky adjustment. Examples are acting out behaviorally, or doing the complete opposite by shutting down and never opening up to receive needed help to get through the process in a healthy manner.

Planning now how you'll cope with your emotions will make a positive difference in your life.

SECTION 2.3

Utilizing The Resources Around You To Help With Your Transition

In this next section, we have two goals:

1. To explore ideas for a smooth, positive transition versus a painful and challenging one
2. To identify how the resources around you can contribute to your successful transition

Social workers, Family Services professionals, and temporary living facilities can be very useful in helping families move through transition with useful tools and resources, such as:

- Referrals for therapy, counseling, or psychiatry
- An advocate who will guide you in a positive direction throughout your transition
- A Life Coach who can help you adjust to your new or changing environment
- Communication with outside family members to fill the void of having no family contact
- Facility personnel to address concerns or obstacles preventing you from adjusting to your new environment
- Special approvals to seek outside services (school, work, extracurricular activities, etc.)
- Help setting goals for reuniting with your parents and loved ones

Changes caused by separation from family members are often traumatizing, especially to children. Allowing trusted people to help you will increase your chances for a smoother, more positive transition. Besides, that's what they're there for—*to help you*.

One of the biggest challenges in getting the *right* kind of help is to ask around. Children or youth in transition may find it difficult to use the help given to them. They tend to harbor things or deal with them internally, which is ***not*** the way to get and use proper help.

💡 This exercise is your opportunity to write down what you would ask each of the resources helping you through your transition. Use this exercise as practice for when you speak with them directly.

SOCIAL WORKER / FAMILY SERVICES

These are the things I'm struggling with while going through transition:

_____

_____

How can you help me during my transition?

_____

_____

This is what would make my transition better:

_____

_____

How kids adjust to their new environment heavily depends on how the facility is operated: how it's run, what rules are in place, what programs are offered, etc.

In my book, *Life in Its Rawest Form*, I talk about my first transition experience away from my home and family. It could have been a better one that led to a smoother transition. For instance, the shelter felt like a detention center, and I felt like I was being punished for something I had no control over. Rules and programs prevented me from living a normal life with some freedoms. I started on the lowest level, which carried fewer privileges (such as television, phone, recreation time), and I had to earn my way to a higher level. We were divided, and I was isolated from the other girls living there. This caused me to feel alone and inferior to the other girls, because they were on a higher level than me.

If I could change things, I would make everyone feel like they were a part of the solution and not the problem. I would create an environment where the residents felt safe, in a home away from home.

If you could talk to the director of the facility, what things about yourself would you share? Reply to each statement below as if you were speaking to that person at this very moment.

GROUP HOME / FOSTER HOME PERSONNEL

These are the things I'm struggling with while going through transition:
___
___
___
___

These are the things preventing me from easily adjusting to my new living environment:
___
___
___

Here is how I would change this new living arrangement so that it would make my stay more comfortable:
___
___
___

These are the things that would make my stay at the group home or foster home more meaningful:
___
___
___

What can you do to help me achieve this?
___
___
___

Here is what I hope to gain from going through this experience while I'm here:
___
___
___
___
___

If the resources that could help your transition were not identified above, list them here along with any questions, concerns, or recommendations you have that can help with your successful and positive transition.

OTHER RESOURCES

Name the resource and how it can help you during your transition:

_____
_____
_____
_____
_____
_____

What concerns regarding your transition would you like to share with this other resource?

_____
_____
_____
_____
_____
_____

What do you want to say to your parents or loved ones while you all are going through transition?

_____
_____
_____
_____
_____
_____

Transitions caused by a family crisis are difficult to deal with. Separation from your parents and siblings can be heart-wrenching, especially when your family is all that you have.

Family Services, group homes, and foster homes all play a pivotal role in how well you adjust to your new environment. They have access to resources that can support you as you get acclimated. Their goal is to make your transition as painless as possible by making you feel at home. The message that should come across, loud and clear, is that the child or youth is part of the solution and not the problem. The people operating these facilities can help convey that message by having supportive programs and standard operating procedures in place.

Too often, children and youth are not helped to understand the magnitude of the problems, which are the sole reason for being there. This causes confusion and frustration, which triggers negative emotions and behaviors. It's vital that the appropriate support and services are made available to help you. These services can help you manage your emotions effectively, thereby avoiding conflict or behavior challenges.

CHAPTER 3

TEENAGE PREGNANCY

Over the last several decades, teen pregnancy has become epidemic. It's more common in communities where poverty is high, where educational success rates are low, and where there is a high percentage of single-parent and dysfunctional households.

Several factors contribute to this problem, and my story is just one of many.

Like many other teenage girls, I came from a broken, dysfunctional home, where I was raised mostly by a single parent. My mother suffered from substance addiction, which significantly impacted my growing-up years.

Her lifestyle made it easier for me to do things I had no business doing at such an early age, such as having unprotected sex and becoming a mother at the age of 15. I, too, was accountable and responsible, because I knew I was making poor choices, even after I knew the consequences and risks. What I didn't have was someone who encouraged me regularly to abstain from premarital sex. I didn't have someone to show me a different direction that would have left less time and room for making poor choices and taking unnecessary risks. There was no guarantee those things wouldn't have happened anyway, but having that role model in my life could have lowered the chances. Having positive support from others, along with extracurricular activities, could have made a difference in my life.

My goal in this section is to show you opportunities for getting the help and support I wasn't fortunate enough to have, to prevent or lessen your becoming an adolescent parent. We'll explore methods for prevention, and we'll help you, if you're already an adolescent parent, with options that offer a brighter future. Some of the topics we'll cover are:

PREVENTIVE MEASURES

- Ways to prevent teenage pregnancy
- Love and relationships without sex
- Using time constructively

ACKNOWLEDGMENT

- Acknowledge the reason(s) you became a parent
- Understand the consequences
- Know the impact to you and others

DEFEATING THE ODDS

- A plan for a brighter future
- Better decision making
- Overcoming obstacles early on
- Not letting your current situation define your future

BREAKING THE CYCLE

- Dare to be different
- Learn from your past
- Be an example to others
- Do not let your surroundings influence you

FIGURE 1

SECTION 3.1

Preventive Measures

Due to the alarming, ever-growing numbers of teen pregnancies in the past several decades, more preventive measures to slow down this precipitous trend are becoming available. Schools, organizations, and communities are playing an instrumental role in helping today's youth. In fact, this widespread movement has evolved into a social responsibility, rather than an individual cause. We stand as a united front in this responsibility to improve individual lives and the overall health of our country.

Preventive measures come in many forms. Second to abstinence is the testimony from adolescent parents who tell of their day-to-day struggles and long-term effects. Hearing their stories, *alone*, is enough to make youth think twice about becoming a parent too soon.

Such a testament is all the reason that youth need to conscientiously avoid sex and/or having babies. These adolescent parents' struggles are *real and unsettling*. Abstinence is a popular cliché as it relates to this topic, and it is **the most effective method** for preventing pregnancy and the life-long road to other problems that result from it.

If I had the opportunity for a redo, I would have used preventive measures. Had I known then what I know now about the struggles that lay ahead for me as a teenage mother, and the impact being a teenage mother would have on my child's life and mine, I would never have considered putting myself in that position. I'd like to think I would have realized how irresponsible and selfish it was to put an innocent life through a multitude of future undue hardships.

If I could do it over, I would have become a mother *after* I was married and had more life experience and financial stability. That way, I wouldn't have spent large chunks of time away from my child while working to secure a better future for us. My child was raised by his father and relatives during my absence. Financial stability would have changed all of that.

The goal for these exercises is to explore choices and opportunities available to you to help avoid *teen pregnancy*, if it's not already too late. The exercises are interactive and thought-provoking.

As an adolescent parent, I've learned there are no black or white answers for this topic. Preventive measures vary, depending on circumstances, resources, environment, and other factors.

What is most important is that you choose the best-fit, realistic methods for your situation and circumstances.

Use the chart below to describe the pros and cons of adolescent parenting. Think about loved ones and others who would be affected by your decision.

List what you stand to gain or lose by choosing to become a parent as a minor. Then summarize your answers at the end of the table. For example, I completed the first table to give you an idea of the effects of becoming a parent at age 15 and how it affected my life.

WHAT YOU HAVE TO LOSE	WHAT YOU HAVE TO GAIN	WHO BENEFITS	WHO SUFFERS
I stand to lose my youth	I gain the experience of parenthood	The parents	The child
I stand to lose opportunities	I gain someone who will love me unconditionally	Family members of both parents	The parents
I stand to lose part of my free will	I gain hardship and more problems		Immediate family members and loved ones
I stand to lose meaningful relationships	I gain the responsibility of another life, in addition to mine, as a minor		
I stand to lose my friends	I gain codependency of others		
I stand to lose sight of my dreams			

Summary of the pros and cons:

- I stand to lose out on my youth and will be forced to mature sooner than my time.
- I could potentially lose opportunities that would afford me a brighter future or useful experiences.
- My struggles as a mother will affect the well-being of my child.
- My immediate family will be impacted as I will depend on their help and support.
- I may not be able to carry out my future dreams as a young mother.
- I become codependent of others and/or the system for help raising my child.
- I no longer have the freedom of living for myself.
- I will create a long road of hardship and problems as I struggle to care for my child.

Now it's your turn:

WHAT YOU HAVE TO LOSE	WHAT YOU HAVE TO GAIN	WHO BENEFITS	WHO SUFFERS

Please note: Additional space to continue this exercise can be found in Appendix C.

Summary of the pros and cons:

_____
_____
_____
_____
_____
_____

If the cons outweigh the pros, you have a clear indication that bringing a child into this world while you're a minor is not the best idea for yourself, the child, and those around you. It can be an impediment to your future, as well as to your child's.

Always consider the difficulties you would place on those around you, as well as the unborn child.

SECTION 3.2

Abstinence, Celibacy, And Contraceptives

Practicing abstinence and/or celibacy is easier said than done, especially in today's society where premarital sex is typical. In times past, society expected us to marry first, *then* have children.

Abstinence not only holds merit religiously and morally, but it also has significant value in preventing teen pregnancy. Sex is a natural milestone for most romantic relationships. The key is to wait for that special someone to share it with.

Looking back, I wish I had thought this way before making irresponsible choices. I now realize how precious that very first moment is, and how important it is to feel confident that this person is someone you can spend forever with. I believe it takes growing together, and having the maturity and wisdom to understand if you are with that special someone.

I hope you'll use experiences I shared in *Life In Its Rawest Form* to make informed decisions about when to have sex and with whom. Hopefully my struggles as a teenage mother will provide examples for why it is important to wait. More important than having sex is to get to know that person better.

💡 List things you can do in a relationship that don't involve sexual activity.

_____
_____
_____
_____
_____
_____
_____
_____
_____
_____
_____
_____
_____

Please note: *Additional space to continue this exercise can be found in Appendix C.*

Enjoying nonsexual activities together helps your relationship grow stronger, because it challenges you to be open-minded and think outside the box for ways to enjoy your time together and build a happy, intriguing relationship without having sexual intercourse.

As your relationship grows, you'll reach a milestone where you'll consent to having sexual intercourse. By that time, you'll have built a solid foundation for a long and sustained relationship.

The key is to abstain while you're going through this important stage of learning and knowing your partner. This solid foundation positions you to endure change and grow stronger as you grow together.

One of the beneficial advantages of abstinence and celibacy, as a youth, teenager, or adult, is building a solid foundation for a long-term relationship. The advantages will vary, since every relationship is different.

In this exercise, identify some of the advantages of practicing abstinence and celibacy. The goal is to highlight the benefits for your life and your relationship. You'll also highlight the disadvantages of not practicing abstinence and celibacy.

In the left column below, list several advantages for practicing abstinence and celibacy for youth and teenagers. In the right column, list several disadvantages when youth and teenagers do NOT practice abstinence and celibacy.

ADVANTAGES	DISADVANTAGES

Please note: *Additional space to continue this exercise can be found in Appendix C.*

It's ***extremely important*** that you put this information to good use by making smarter choices early on and before it's too late.

Change in relationships, for better or for worse, is inevitable. They never stay the same. Introducing new situations and experiences, like sex, influences the type of change that will take place. Sex will cause a relationship to change—for the good or for the bad. Consider what's at stake before having sex too soon, and whether it's worth the risk of compromising the relationship.

No two relationships are the same. Even if you see others taking risks, that doesn't mean the risks you take will have the same outcome. However, there are common risks that apply to any relationship.

In the next exercise, you'll identify potential risks from having adolescent premarital sex. Your goal is to help yourself make informed decisions beforehand.

What are the risks associated with having <u>pre</u>marital sex versus <u>post</u>marital sex?

PREMARITAL	POSTMARITAL

Now consider the risks you've identified. Are they greater risks when engaging in premarital sex versus waiting until you're married? Will this information help you make informed decisions based on the likely outcome of your choice? While there may be no set timeline or rule for how long you should wait, abstinence means not doing these things until you and your partner have decided when that will be.

Practicing abstinence or celibacy is one of THE best investments you could ever make for your future. Waiting for the "right" person and uniting in marriage is, for me, the best possible way to invest in a happy future. In hindsight, one of the most important lessons I learned after several unsuccessful attempts at love is that the key to a successful relationship is being with that "right" person. I wish I had thought this way early on: ensuring, as much as possible, that the person embodies the qualities I strongly believe in and desire ***before*** becoming intimate. However, it's not too late.

Recognizing when you have that "Ms. or Mr. Right" is based on your interpretation. What "right" means to me may not mean what "right" means to you. This is an extremely important step: **Know what qualities you're looking for in a partner, and what expectations or standards that person must meet, before deciding the time is right for a long-term commitment.**

In this exercise, we'll explore the qualities you're looking for in the "right" person. I'll start off with qualities I look for. Then it's your turn.

QUALITIES I LOOK FOR IN A COMPANION
✓ Can I fall utterly in love with this person?
✓ Do most of our morals and values align with one another?
✓ Can I trust this person?
✓ Do I know enough about this person to commit to a long-term or intimate relationship?
✓ Is this person goal-oriented, ambitious, and driven to succeed?
✓ Is this person stable and financially secure, or does this person have a plan to achieve stability and security?
✓ Is the person honest and loyal?
✓ Is the person kind, funny, and intelligent?
✓ Is this someone I would want my children to model themselves after?

Your turn! List some of the qualities you look for in a companion:

QUALITIES I LOOK FOR IN A COMPANION
✓
✓
✓
✓
✓
✓
✓
✓
✓
✓

Please note: Additional space to continue this exercise can be found in Appendix C.

Clearly, abstinence does not guarantee that a relationship won't change for the worse, but marriage, or waiting to have sex until you're confident you are with that special someone, will **lessen** the chances of your relationships going wrong because of sex.

It's not possible to be 100% certain about a person. We all take risks. However, doing lots of due diligence up front will have a positive difference later. Identifying and understanding the qualities and expectations you want will help you know if a person is compatible, which can prevent heartache and loss of time.

Unfortunately, teens having premarital sex is the sad reality of the world we live in. Sex happens, even with all the support that encourages abstinence.

Practicing safe sex is important. Contraceptives can prevent teen pregnancy. There are numerous forms of contraceptives for males and females. Look into the resources available to help you choose the best options.

Be sure to make this the very first step: discuss sex and ways to prevent pregnancy with your parents or legal guardians ***before*** making any decisions about birth control.

Birth control and contraceptives are not 100% effective, either, so there is still the possibility of becoming pregnant due to improper use, defective devices, irregular use, and more. However, chances of pregnancy are significantly less if used correctly.

A relationship's dynamics will change once sex is introduced. The change can be good or bad. Sexually active youth risk a number of unforeseen problems that can have significant, long-term effects. One of the most impactful, of course, is pregnancy; however, pregnancy will likely only add to other major problems.

Having a baby as a teenager will complicate your life. What once was a normal, simple life of a teenager suddenly becomes a life of hardship and turmoil. You no longer have the luxury of caring only for yourself. Immediately you've become responsible for another person's life. Your needs and wants become secondary to your child's needs and wants.

Teen parenthood also complicates your relationships and friendships, because your top priority is your child.

Adolescent parenting creates hardships and personal struggles. Financial stability, child support, co-parenting—they all bring undo stress to a relationship, which naturally lead to tension or resentment in your partner.

Your problems now become the problems that an adult deals with, although you aren't legally of age yet. ***Life as you once new it no longer exists!***

Practicing safe sex isn't just about abstinence. It's about being responsible and taking precautions against becoming a parent. It's also about accountability, and not involving yourself in activities too advanced for your age group, or that put you at risk for becoming an adolescent parent.

An often overlooked aspect of teen pregnancy is that it can have a negative effect on the child's life, because of the hardships caused by your age and inexperience. More often than not, financial stability and independence require that you're legally of age. It's nearly impossible to provide this for yourself or your child as a teen. Therefore, the child suffers, as well as you, the parent(s).

This state of financial instability and lack of independence can last until you become of legal age, when you can provide a stable income. *Hence*, this is why it's so important that you do not become an adolescent parent.

In this exercise, first list several advantages of practicing safe sex, especially as a teenager; and, second, several disadvantages resulting from not practicing safe sex. This exercise will open your eyes a little wider to the risks of unsafe sex. You'll also learn preventive measures if you are sexually active.

ADVANTAGES	DISADVANTAGES

Please note: *Additional space to continue this exercise can be found in Appendix C.*

This information is exactly why it's important to responsibly practice safe sex. Although it's best to have NO sex while you're an adolescent, the reality is, it would be much worse to become pregnant at this time of your life. Because premarital sex puts you at risk for so many things that can go wrong, it's really not worth risking. If you don't practice safe sex for yourself, do it for the lives of others, and potentially for the life of an unborn child.

SECTION 3.3

Using Time Constructively

One of the many reasons youth get involved in things they shouldn't is, they have too much idle time and nothing constructive to fill the time. Typically, they have more time available, because they have fewer responsibilities and obligations than adults.

Thus, teenage pregnancy results from not having something constructive to do—something that empowers teens, captures their interest, and leaves little time for sexual activity. Some communities provide opportunities for teens to enjoy structured activities, and, The Search Institute says, fewer youth engage in risk-taking behaviors—Blyth, 1992 (https://thenationalcampaign.org/sites/default/files/resource-primarydownload/GetOrganized_0.pdf).

There are lots of activities to choose from, such as:

- Volunteer work
- Church activities
- Reading and learning
- Creating new hobbies
- Traveling
- Spending time with family and friends
- Exercising
- Outreach programs
- Summer Jobs
- Community service

Most worthwhile programs encourage responsible and positive behaviors that help you remain qualified. These stipulations can serve as preventive measures against teen pregnancy, because they incentivize you to demonstrate responsible behavior, which, in turn, encourages you to make better choices. Ultimately, these programs decrease the likelihood of youth becoming teen parents.

If you aspire to further your education, or have interest in a specific career, take advantage of training programs offering opportunities. Programs like these heighten interests and increase focus on building skills, allowing less time to focus on sexual relationships.

Tracking your schedule helps create structure in your life. A tracking plan provides guidance and direction on how to better manage your time. It leaves little room for uncertainty on how to spend your time or what to do next. A plan will create a daily regimen for you and lessen your time spent on high-risk activities.

In the next exercise, create your own chart. Track weekly and monthly commitments, then use this information to plan your days to maximize your time for constructive activities. The plan can also help prevent idle time.

HERE IS AN EXAMPLE OF A MONTHLY ACTIVITY PLAN:

WEEK 1	ACTIVITY:						
	SUNDAY	MONDAY	TUESDAY	WEDNESDAY	THURSDAY	FRIDAY	SATURDAY
	TIME:	TIME:	TIME:	TIME:	TIME:	TIME:	TIME:

WEEK 2	ACTIVITY:						
	SUNDAY	MONDAY	TUESDAY	WEDNESDAY	THURSDAY	FRIDAY	SATURDAY
	TIME:	TIME:	TIME:	TIME:	TIME:	TIME:	TIME:

WEEK 3	ACTIVITY:						
	SUNDAY	MONDAY	TUESDAY	WEDNESDAY	THURSDAY	FRIDAY	SATURDAY
	TIME:	TIME:	TIME:	TIME:	TIME:	TIME:	TIME:

WEEK 4	ACTIVITY:						
	SUNDAY	MONDAY	TUESDAY	WEDNESDAY	THURSDAY	FRIDAY	SATURDAY
	TIME:	TIME:	TIME:	TIME:	TIME:	TIME:	TIME:

Please note: *Additional space to continue this exercise can be found in Appendix C.*

Youth and teens who are involved in extracurricular activities, studies show, are more likely to graduate, and less likely to become teen parents. To help disadvantaged youth and teens at risk, more programs are being funded on a national level. These programs and opportunities are not a cure for teen pregnancy, but they do make a substantial difference in teen pregnancy rates.

Community and outreach programs are designed to help youth utilize their full potential. But the biggest help comes from parents. Parents are accountable and responsible for ensuring that their children find opportunities that set them up for success. The more we commit to this, the better off our teens and youth will be.

SECTION 3.4

Adolescent Parenting

One of the biggest challenges I have faced in my entire life is becoming a mother at the age of 15.

…Nothing came easy and everything was a struggle…

One night of romance literally changed my life—good and bad—forever.

Life as I knew it changed drastically when I gave birth to my son. He was and is the love of my life. But loving him as I do didn't prepare me for the future we faced together.

Becoming a mother at age 15 began a long road of hardship and adversity. Every day was a challenge, even with his father's support. I hadn't given any thought to the realities before becoming pregnant at age 14. I didn't think about the risks of having sex too soon—unprotected sex. I knew very little about birth control, something I had never discussed with my mother or any adult.

Once you become a teenage parent, life changes. It's more difficult to be a teen parent than an adult parent. The reason is, teenagers are not of legal age to work in a job that affords an adequate income to support a quality life. And, teens simply haven't lived long enough to know how to properly raise a child.

There is so much to life teenagers have yet to learn and experience. Having a child as a teenager is an impediment, in most cases, and prevents you from living the optimal teenage life.

I know about these impediments firsthand. I was still coming of age, trying to figure out life. Becoming a mother, I missed out on learning many things about life. The moment I became pregnant, I was catapulted into adulthood. I had to sacrifice doing what I wanted to do with friends, because I had a child to care for, or I had to go to work. Outside of caring for my child and working, I was too tired to do anything with friends.

When my son was born, I was in utter bliss. Nothing had ever made me feel so happy and complete. I wanted to protect him and give him a better life than the life I had growing up.

But I faced many challenges. Not many job opportunities were open to me, a 15-year-old, to earn a decent wage. Since I wasn't legally old enough to work full-time, my only choices were part-time jobs. I was barely old enough to earn minimum wage, so I had to take whatever pay they offered me.

Some of my struggles were:

- Learning how to care for a baby
- Finding a job that paid well and with benefits for my son and me
- Getting adequate rest, especially at night
- Finding time for myself
- Hanging out and going places without taking my baby
- Using all of the money I earned to buy diapers, baby food, and other childcare needs
- Feeling ashamed and judged by others
- Seeing the light at the end of the tunnel

At the tender age of 15, I felt like I had the responsibilities of the world on my shoulders. I wanted this feeling to go away as quickly as possible. Before I could change it, I knew I had to live responsibly.

Outside of raising my son, my focus was to keep a job and complete high school. It was my only solution to lightening this burden that weighed me down as a young mother. I had very little room for error, and I could not lose focus. This meant I set goals that would afford my son and me a better quality of life.

As time went on, things got a little easier. I established a normal cadence, such as caring for my son, going to school, working. Without a college degree, no matter where I worked, I knew the financial outcome would be the same. To earn more would require a college degree, or even two. I promised myself that my financial hardship would be temporary until I completed college.

Once you have a child, it's your parental duty and obligation to give your child the highest quality of life possible. It doesn't mean being rich or wealthy. It means being able to sustain financial stability and security until they reach legal age.

Your goal as an adolescent parent is to ask for and use help as a ***temporary vehicle*** until you become self-sufficient. It's okay to ask for assistance while you work toward your goal, which is, hopefully, to build a brighter future for you and your family. Always have an end date in mind when using outside help.

We'll get more into setting goals and strategizing in **Chapter 4: Setting Goals and Executing Them**. For now, let's explore things you should be thinking about as a teenage parent to make your life and your child's life better.

The point of this exercise is to think about your current situation and the challenges keeping you from a better quality of life for your child or children. Take a good look at your situation and identify opportunities for improvement. You may want to consider things that:

- Challenge you on a regular basis
- Limit you due to your age or legal status
- Help you improve your circumstances
- Present you with an option of doing them differently in the meantime

CHALLENGES

Describe below some of the difficulties you face on a regular basis as a teenage parent:

1. _____
_____
_____
_____
_____
_____
_____

2. _____
_____
_____
_____
_____
_____
_____

3. _____
_____
_____
_____
_____
_____
_____

ROOT CAUSE

Now explain the root cause for issues you described above. Are they issues attributed to your age? If "yes," does your age hinder you from getting a well-paying job that provides financial stability? Does your age prevent you from going to college at this time? Does being a teenage parent prevent you from providing a stable home for you and your child?

4. _____
_____
_____

5. _____
_____
_____

IDENTIFY HELP NEEDED

Based on the challenges and their root cause you described in the two exercises above, identify below what would help make them less challenging. List any people or resources that would help you improve each situation or challenge.

6. _____
_____
_____
_____

7. _____
_____
_____
_____

8. _____
_____
_____
_____

SECTION 3.5

Making Adjustments—Doing Things Differently

Several of my challenges, as a teenage mother, were similar to yours, where I had to make adjustments and accommodations to provide basic necessities. Sometimes I had to choose more affordable alternatives. Finding affordable alternatives became a natural way of life for me, as I struggled to make ends meet. If I couldn't afford to buy something my baby or I needed, I'd think of less-expensive substitutes. Sometimes it came down to going without for the time being. As an adolescent mother, this became my reality and way of life.

The purpose of this exercise is to think differently and make adjustments to sustain financial stability, as much as possible, while providing an adequate life for you and your child. As a teenage parent, you have fewer options for earning an income. The income you earn now, with no college education, will not be remotely enough to support a proper living for your family.

That's why it's important to think differently to make adjustments and sacrifices until you're older and can provide a better life.

In previous exercises, you've described day-to-day challenges in providing for you and your child. You've identified the root cause for these challenges, which is, very likely, connected to your age and level of education. You've described resources that could help you improve your situation until you become of age, when you'll have better opportunities for improving your situation.

In this section, describe life changes that would help the issues you've described in previous exercises.

What could you do differently that would allow you to still meet the needs of you and your child while cutting costs?

1. _____
_____
_____
_____

2. _____
_____
_____
_____

3. _____
_____
_____
_____

Use information from the exercises above to improve your situation in the best way possible. They're temporary solutions that will minimize the common challenges of being a teenage parent. As we learned, there aren't many options that will afford you financial security, so this information should be used to help until you come of age and pursue better opportunities.

Success doesn't happen overnight. It takes time, patience, and dedication. Investing in higher education and building a career seems like it will take a long time, but the outcome is well worth your effort and time.

Life may be tough for the first couple years of adolescent parenting, but, truly, they are ***only as hard as you make them***. Living responsibly and making smarter choices will make a difference in the level of challenges you have. Give it your all to lessen the impact of these issues. Be determined to improve your situation by setting goals and making plans for your brighter future.

The first step is to set goals, long-term and short-term. It's what we'll do in **Chapter 4: Setting Goals and Executing Them.**

SECTION 3.6

Two Teenaged Parents Are Better Than One

If I'd known then what I know now, I would have worked harder to keep my relationship with my son's father sex-free for a longer time.

If I'd known then what I know now, I would have looked into birth control options once our relationship got more serious.

If I'd known then what I know now, I would have explored options other than having sex to build a stronger relationship and foundation.

I robbed myself of having a successful relationship because I **didn't** do these things.

Today, like me, millions of teenagers have robbed themselves of a fulfilling, successful, and long-term relationship with someone because they had sex prematurely. They, too, did not give their relationships enough time to acquire the proper tools and resources to adequately prepare for the life-changing event of having a baby.

Having a baby as a teenager forces the relationship full throttle into parenthood, where you no longer have the luxury of taking your time to get to know one another or spending time one-on-one. The dynamic of the relationship changes drastically. Your goals become all about how you can both provide financial security and stability, medical benefits, and childcare while tending to school and work. The relationship takes on a whole new set of problems than before.

Having both parents involved in the child's life is equally important for teenage parents as it is for adult parents. Optimize your relationship as best as you can. It doesn't mean giving up hope of having that dream relationship. It does mean working hard to still make it happen. "Two is better than one" is a popular cliché that holds true in this case.

Even with extreme challenges and difficulties, having each other for support will make a significant difference. When both parents partner to raise their child, they increase the chances for a successful relationship, because the responsibility and pressure doesn't fall solely on one person. The load is equally shared, which often has a positive effect on your relationship, as well as on your child's life.

The dynamic of your relationship changes when you become a parent too young. The overwhelming stress and responsibility can cause your relationship to deteriorate. Very likely, you'll have to put on hold the things you did before becoming parents, so that your child's needs are put first.

As a result, this can have a negative impact on your relationship if you're not conscientiously aware and taking precautions to prevent your relationship from deteriorating. *If* it comes to you both raising the child apart, it's important to keep the other parent in mind, as well as your goals for a successful parenting relationship. Chances for maintaining an intact family unit increase, while potentially strengthening your bond as parents.

Explore ways to function as one unit while strengthening your bond as young parents, companions, and partners.

FIGURE 2

Figure 2 suggests ways to strengthen your bond as adolescent parents. But it's never a one-size-fits-all situation. Your relationship goals will vary, depending on your own circumstances.

💡 In the exercise below, define the importance of co-parenting, and how you'll build an even better relationship, in spite of becoming parents too soon. Feel free to list ways you'll work together as parents, while strengthening your companionship.

_____
_____
_____
_____
_____
_____
_____
_____
_____
_____
_____
_____
_____
_____
_____
_____
_____
_____
_____

Typically, when both parents raise a child, you instill healthy relationship and family values. You also improve your child(s) future relationships. Growing up in an intact family and seeing their parents' togetherness creates stability and security in the child's life. It also sets a positive example that they're more likely to pass on to their family some day. The child also suffers fewer of the usual "adolescent parent" misfortunes.

Having both parents together won't take away the hardships your child or children will encounter; however, having both parents does lessen the direct impact on the child.

SECTION 3.7

Breaking The Cycle

It's no secret that teenage parents, particularly mothers, have less chance of succeeding in life. Parenthood becomes an impediment to a brighter future. *If they had any* hopes and dreams of becoming educated professionals, that picture of success becomes only a figment of their imagination. Stereotypically, they drop out of school, go on welfare, and receive public housing benefits. They have more children while still teenagers and they break up with the father(s), leaving them alone to raise their child/children.

According to Dosometing.org, parenthood is the leading reason that teen girls drop out of school. More than 50% of teen mothers never graduate from high school (https://www.dosomething.org/us/facts/11-facts-about-teen-pregnancy).

About 25% of teen moms have a second child within 24 months of the birth of their first baby (https://www.dosomething.org/us/facts/11-facts-about-teen-pregnancy). Fewer than 2% of teen moms earn a college degree by age 30 (https://www.dosomething.org/us/facts/11-facts-about-teen-pregnancy).

Eight out of 10 teen dads don't marry the mother of their child (https://www.dosomething.org/us/facts/11-facts-about-teen-pregnancy).

More than half of all mothers on welfare had their first child as a teenager. In fact, two-thirds of families begun by a young, unmarried mother are poor (https://www.dosomething.org/us/facts/11-facts-about-teen-pregnancy).

It should be no surprise that impoverished communities, where teenage pregnancy and adolescent parenting exists, have limited opportunities, meaning that the likelihood of a successful future is scarce, unless a person is motivated to succeed and looks beyond their surroundings. In these communities, it's all too common for these parents to have a poor work ethic, discontinue their education, or even believe that they can have a better life. They've become accustomed to a lifestyle of impoverished thinking and behavior. Routinely, these parents become welfare recipients, or they receive some type of government assistance until their children are too old to qualify any longer.

Statistics show that over half of them drop out of school and lose all hope of going to college. The responsibility of being a teenage parent is either too overwhelming or too challenging. They find it easier to give up school and work, rather than to stay the course until things get better.

These parents, unfortunately, do not have the fight and power they need in order to withstand the obstacles associated with adolescent parenting, nor do they have a good support system to cheer them on and encourage them to keep going. Why? Mainly, because those around them lack this helpful support system themselves.

Teenage parents commonly believe it's easier to sit back and wait on the government, or others, to take care of them and their child/children, rather than work to support themselves. To increase their government benefits, sometimes they'll have more children.

This infectious thinking has plagued teenage parents living in impoverished communities throughout our nation. It is a problem wherever there is a high concentration of poverty, low education rates, and where opportunities are scarce—making it all the easier to lose hope when nothing in their lives inspires or encourages them to be great.

Which stereotype or statistic will *you* work hard not to become? How will *you* plan to avoid becoming another statistic?

In the next several sections, we'll get into the common lifestyles teenage parents fall into. The goal is to help you identify an approach that will break this vicious cycle.

More often than not, teenage mothers will give birth to a second or third child while still an adolescent. Statistics in this report, (https://www.cdc.gov/vitalsigns/teenpregnancy/), show that 86% of teen pregnancies are second births. That's nearly one in every five teen pregnancies between the ages of 15 and 19! This alarming cycle has become common for various reasons.

The purpose of this section of *Teen Pregnancy* is to help you break this cycle of repeating the same poor choices or mistakes. Hopefully you'll be enlightened to make better decisions the second, *sometimes third and fourth*, time around.

An important piece in breaking the cycle is to understand why you decided in the first place to have kids so early. What was your purpose or reason? Perhaps your answer will help uncover issues that need addressing. Then, as an alternative to having children, and as a solution to the problem(s), create opportunities to get help.

As mentioned earlier, teen parents have various reasons for having multiple children. Each situation may be different, but common variables include, but are not limited to:

1. Being influenced by what they see around them on a day-to-day basis
2. Lacking proper experience with the first child
3. Lacking the understanding and experience of what is necessary to effectively parent a child
4. Being the norm for their environment and community
5. Using it as a way and means to access financial resources (such as Public Aid)
6. Believing that having a baby will strengthen their relationship
7. Filling a void, thus providing happiness and the feeling of being needed

If any of the reasons given above fit your situation, list the item number in the OPTION spaces below. Then review each item to acknowledge your awareness of why you feel you need to have children at your young age. Then, in the DESCRIPTION column, write a simple statement that describes how this item fits your situation.

If none of points 1-7 on the previous page relate to your situation, skip to the statements under the table to describe your own reasons.

OPTION	DESCRIPTION

Specify the reason(s) you decided to become a teen parent.

_____
_____
_____

What do you hope to gain or get from having a child as a teenager?

_____
_____
_____

Is it possible you chose to become a parent to mask other problems or pain going on in your life? Being aware of this will allow you to address the issue(s) and open the door to seek the help you need.

Being aware can also prevent repeating the same choices. Ask the hard questions that will help you make better choices in the future. Your answers will help you to understand the reasons that played a part in your current predicament. This knowledge is power for lessening the chances of repeating the same choices that keep you from being the best you can be.

TEENAGE PREGNANCY | 65

SECTION 3.8

Being Accountable And Taking Responsibility As A Teenage Parent

As stated previously, being a teenage parent is more challenging than being a parent as an adult. Adults have more options for building financial security and stability. As a teenage parent, you put yourself and your child/children through hardships and oppression because of your age and the limitations that keep you from enjoying a decent quality of life.

Therefore, lessening hardships is extremely important. It's even more important to make immediate changes for the better, and invest a considerable amount of time pursuing short-term and long-term goals. ***This helps speed up your path to success***. You'll struggle less, and it will leave less room for errors like these:

- Repeating mistakes that led you to getting pregnant
- Putting off decisions regarding plans for college and career choices
- Having multiple children while still a teenager or adolescent
- Getting involved with the wrong person(s) that lead to making poor choices

Parenting is a serious and enormous responsibility, no matter what your age. You must discipline yourself to make smarter choices, set goals, and achieve them. Doing this regularly can save you, your child/children, and your loved ones from hardships, heartache, and trouble. You don't have to be perfect (and you will make mistakes along the way), but resilience and consistency will take you a long way. I can't encourage you enough about this—the sooner you get focused on building a brighter future and working toward your goals, the sooner you'll improve your life and the lives of your child or children.

In my book, I said, **"I couldn't give up or look back, because no one else had my back. The more I understood that, the more I pushed myself to work harder each day."** And, **"As overwhelming as it could sometimes be, *failure was not an option.*"**

I literally took this mantra to heart. My daily struggles were enough to make me realize I couldn't go down the same path that had led me to the situation I was in.

- The only way to improve my situation was to stay focused on completing high school, ***on time***, and plan on attending college immediately after high school graduation.
- Meanwhile, I had to look for a job that offered the highest compensation and benefits, according to my age and circumstances.
- Between going to school and caring for my son, I worked as many hours as possible, so I could provide a decent living for us.
- Through all of this, I ***could not*** lose focus to complete college.
- Having a college degree or two was the best way to provide financial security and stability for my son and me.
- Financial security and stability would also lessen the hardships and stress I lived with as a teenage mother.

Next, describe how you'll be accountable and responsible as a teenage parent.

How will you ensure that *failure is not an option*?

_____
_____
_____
_____

What is your plan for taking full accountability and responsibility to ensure that you make the best of your situation while fulfilling your goals for a brighter future for you and your child/children?

_____
_____
_____
_____

What can you do to position yourself for this brighter future?

1. _____
2. _____
3. _____
4. _____
5. _____
6. _____
7. _____
8. _____
9. _____
10. _____

SECTION 3.9

Making Lifestyle Changes To Become A Better Me For My Child

Getting different results may require changes in how we normally do things—the choices we normally make, the people we normally interact with, the environments we normally place ourselves in, and how we normally think. Making these changes could be a part of the solution to break the cycle of repeatedly having children as a teenager.

Once you recognize the reasons for your actions, you'll be forced to question if you're making the best decisions. Your answer will remind you not to make decisions under certain circumstances if you're trying to not get pregnant again.

When I had my son, I worked as much as possible to provide for him and to help my son's father, so the entire financial burden didn't rest solely on him. Sometimes, I worked a 16-hour-day when my school schedule would permit. I also became solely responsible for my personal financial needs, as I had before becoming a mother. My mother had provided a roof over my head, which was short-lived, at times, and food, on occasion. That was mostly it. For the rest, I had to make it on my own.

The substantial amount of pressures, responsibilities, and obligations changed the way I lived and thought. My son's father and I stayed in our relationship for the first couple of years of our son's life, so I took precautions to not become pregnant again. I could no longer run the streets, as I had in the past. Those **opportunities** to make mistakes and poor decisions hadn't changed, and all it would have taken was for me to put myself in that environment again.

Even though I love my son and I am grateful to have him, I never wanted to put myself and another kid through those struggles. Nor did I want to raise my son under the stereotypical conditions that most teenage mothers in my community lived under. I wanted sole ownership and responsibility for my son's financial well-being. I did not want to sit back and collect welfare checks. I did not want to drop out of school and live in an impoverished environment all day, every day.

To avoid going down the same path as most teenage parents living in my community, I had to think outside the box.

In these next several exercises, explore ways to break the cycle of adolescent parenthood. Define what "breaking the cycle" means to you, and later, create goals that will guide you to break the cycle.

One of the goals for this exercise is to think about how not to repeat the things that put you in this position.

Define below what "breaking the cycle" means to you, but first I will give an example of what this phrase means to me.

	WHAT BREAKING THE CYCLE MEANS TO ME:
1.	Lead by example. Show others that there are opportunities for getting it right the second time around.
2.	Learn from past failures, poor choices, and mistakes.
3.	Work even harder to provide a brighter future for my child and me.
4.	Set goals and create a plan to build a brighter future.
5.	Maintain a positive outlook along the way.
6.	Try not to be discouraged.
7.	Seek positive role models and mentors to help show me a better way.
8.	Don't succumb to obstacles.
9.	Do not put myself in a position to become pregnant, unless my husband and I mutually agree.
10.	Change starts with ME!

Identifying my definition helped keep me from repeating the decisions that led me to teenage motherhood. They helped me to not limit myself because of my circumstances, while reaching for the stars. Thanks to these definitions, I did not allow my situation to derail me from achieving my goals for a successful future.

Your definitions should have a similar purpose. Very likely, they'll be different from mine, but, whatever they are, they should be the catalyst that leads to a better you, a better parent, and to a better, brighter future.

In the space below, define what breaking the cycle means to you. It may only be one definition, or it may be more. There are no right or wrong answers. Your definition(s) should reflect how you can break the cycle of having more children while still a teenager or adolescent, and how you can provide the best quality of life for you and your child/children.

WHAT BREAKING THE CYCLE MEANS TO ME:	
1.	
2.	
3.	
4.	
5.	
6.	
7.	
8.	
9.	
10.	

Please note: *Additional space to continue this exercise can be found in Appendix C.*

SECTION 3.10

Break The Cycle—Choose To Be Different

Now that you've defined your meaning of breaking the cycle, the next step should be to define the steps you'll take to do so.

But first, think about this: Does breaking the cycle apply only to you, or does it also apply to others? If it applies to others, who would they be? Based on your answer, create a plan that will help you and others you've identified. Your plan will consist of ways to alter your lifestyle and a list of things to prevent yourself from repeating past poor choices. The plan you come up with should list ways to avoid following the growing number of teenage parents who have chosen the impoverished route to raise their child/children. Your goal is to identify *how* you'll choose to be different by setting a good example for your child and others, ultimately preventing you from falling into the trap of impoverished teenage parenthood.

Earlier in this chapter, I told you about a report showing that more than 50% of teenage parents—mothers, in particular—end up on welfare, drop out of school, and do not attend college. While various factors play into this, by being better informed and educated on these issues, you'll increase your chances for successfully avoiding the same choices.

During my adolescent parenting years, I decided NOT to be among the more than 50%. I would, instead, be part of the smaller percentage who chose a different, better path: those who chased their dreams of a successful future, regardless of their situation; those who didn't let their circumstances decide their future. I chose to be part of the percentage who worked to provide for their child and not depend on others. Although I was considered a rarity in my community, I would not let that deter me from my chosen path.

Goals I set for myself had to do with what was best for my son. I chose to put his needs before mine. I considered what I hoped to accomplish as a young mother, and what lessons I wanted to teach my son, so he wouldn't repeat my mistakes. I created a plan to break the cycle for my son and me.

In this next exercise, come up with a high-level plan to break the cycle of the more than 50% described above. Include goals you can achieve as an adolescent parent, and goals you can achieve for a successful future for you and your child/children. Then use this plan as your guide and frequently refer to it as you set out on your journey. In **Chapter 4: Setting Goals and Executing Them**, we'll use your plan to break the cycle as part of goal setting.

This table lists the most common statistics and stereotypes already discussed in this chapter on the more than 50% of teenage parents, specifically mothers. To break this cyclical effect, describe how you'll avoid becoming a statistic. I'll go first:

STATISTICS SAY	I SAY	I WILL BREAK THE CYCLE BY
More than 50% of teen mothers never graduate from high school.	I will graduate from high school on time with all of my credits.	1. Managing my duties as a mother and student, so I don't fall behind in either. 2. Tracking my progress closely to ensure I meet all requirements by my expected graduation date. 3. Seeking help if needed to avoid failing and jeopardizing my date.
Around 25% of teen moms have a second child within 24 months of their first child.	I will not have more children as an adolescent or teenager.	1. Fully understanding the choices that put me here. 2. Remaining extremely cautious not to repeat the same choices. 3. Committing to having no more children until I am financially secure, stable, married, and a college graduate.
Fewer than 2% of teen moms earn a college degree by age 30.	I will set goals to start and finish college within 4-5 years from graduating high school.	1. Setting goals to attend college right after graduating high school. 2. Graduating college within the standard time-frame for each degree.
Eight out of 10 teen dads don't marry the mother of their child.	I will not have more children out of wedlock and as a teenager.	1. Vowing to myself not to repeat actions that led me to become an unwed, teenage mother.

I shared my plan for breaking the cycle and avoiding becoming one of the more than 50%. I used this information as a guide to set goals, and as a reference during my journey.

TEENAGE PREGNANCY

In the table below, document your plan for avoiding that more than 50% category mentioned frequently in this chapter. Describe how you'll become a part of the lesser, healthier percentage who expect to break the mold/cycle. Your responses may be different from mine, yet similar in that you're choosing different and better.

STATISTICS SAY	I SAY	I WILL BREAK THE CYCLE BY
More than 50% of teen mothers never graduate from high school.		
Around 25% of teen moms have a second child within 24 months of their first child.		
Fewer than 2% of teen moms earn a college degree by age 30.		
Eight out of 10 teen dads don't marry the mother of their child.		

Please note: *Additional space to continue this exercise can be found in Appendix C.*

Now that we've established ways to not be among the negative statistics and stereotypes associated with teen parenthood, we're well-equipped to make better lives for ourselves by choosing differently.

In this chapter, we were made aware of common paths that more than 50% of teenage parents choose for raising their child/children. These paths lead to low education completion rates, more children born out of wedlock, raising children in poverty, being welfare recipients, and more.

Our goal is to break this cycle by staying accountable and taking ownership in providing a higher quality of life for our children. Set a good example and minimize, as much as possible, the impact on their lives due to teen parenthood. Beat the odds by exceeding expectations and statistics that put us in a box of failure. Use the plan above and stick to it, and set your direction for a better life.

In conclusion…

In this chapter, we covered a lot of territory. We looked at a range of topics relevant in today's society, and we identified ways to optimize our situation as teen parents.

We learned:

- Abstinence and celibacy are the best options in preventing teen pregnancy
- Several preventive measures to becoming teen and adolescent parents
- Various contraceptives can prevent teen pregnancy
- The value of waiting to have sex, and the importance of taking adequate time to know your partner and build a foundation for your relationship
- Constructive use of your time as an adolescent and teenager helps prevent teen pregnancy
- Lifestyle adjustments made by doing things differently can prevent recurring mistakes and poor decisions
- Community and outreach programs have an important impact on teen pregnancy prevention
- Two parents are better than one. This holds true especially as it relates to teen parenthood. Having both parents in the child's life, even when the parents are adolescents, can provide more resources and stability than having only one parent. It helps minimize the hardship the child will suffer due to the parents' adolescence. It also increases the long-term quality of life and sets a good example for the child to see both parents working to overcome adversity together.
- Ways to effectively break the cycle of teen parenthood and choose to avoid its negative perceptions and statistics

Use these topics as guides to improve your life as a teenage parent. The exercises and information revealed a number of common issues and adversities teen parents face in today's society.

The purpose of each topic is to become aware of the challenges, and identify ways to manage them. We've provided several helpful tools and resources for various situations, and they should help influence positive change. In addition, the information shared with you in each topic can drive positive outcomes and statistics.

The ultimate goal for each topic is to inspire and motivate you to work hard at building a brighter future, and to keep you off the path you're already on. When you've completed this chapter, you should be well-informed and able to make wiser choices and healthier decisions for a better quality of life for you and your child/children.

The intent isn't to discourage you from seeking help when you need it. The intent is more to influence you to put your full potential to use to figure things out on your own, as your *first* option. There is nothing wrong with receiving help when needed, as you take these important steps on your new path to a brighter, better future. The key is to not abuse the resources, or take from others who may need them.

Remember that everyone's story is different. We all make mistakes, poor decisions, and judgments from time to time, because no one is perfect. Becoming a parent too soon doesn't make you less significant than anyone else. You have the ability to make better choices in the future.

Breaking the cycle and creating positive change takes hard work and dedication. **Never doubt that it is possible**. Your route may be different from others, and you may encounter more, or fewer, challenges than some—**<u>but it can still be done!</u>** Yes, life will be tougher for a while, but you'll prevail because you have young lives depending on it—even more reason to excel.

The unique thing about being an adolescent parent is that you get to show your children, and others, that it's possible to prevail when statistics and society predict otherwise. You have an opportunity to set an example that *nothing is impossible if you work hard at it.*

*Change starts with **you**!*

CHAPTER 4

SETTING GOALS AND EXECUTING THEM

Wouldn't it be nice if we could have the things we want without having to create a plan to get them? The majority of the people in this world don't have it that easy.

Goal-setting is an integral, important part in living out our dreams. Goals can be short-term or long-term. Short-term goals refer to the near or immediate future, whereas long-term goals mean the future.

There are many reasons to set goals. Each goal will have a separate, different purpose, but its main intent and purpose is to achieve something in an organized and structured way.

Generally, we set goals for things that interest or motivate us, and for things we want to achieve within a certain time-frame. Common goals are:

- Educational
- Career
- Daily
- Financial
- Credit
- Relationship (family, friends, romance)

There are many ways to set goals. It all depends on preference. Some of us set smaller, short-term goals, while others set bigger, long-term goals.

Either is okay. The key is to make the goals attainable.

The main *goal* of this chapter is to *define* goals—short-term and long-term—and develop a plan for executing them. What goes into achieving goals? **Hard work and sacrifices.** We'll also discuss those.

You'll also have exercises to help you come up with ways to achieve your goals, plans to identify sacrifices and lifestyle changes, resources and tools to create strategies, and more. You'll frequently refer to these exercises while you're working toward achieving your dreams.

SECTION 4.1

Making Plans For Your Future

What are your aspirations? Think rationally about your future, so that you can identify ways to improve it. It's an important step. Where you are today is your start for determining future tomorrows. There are endless opportunities. Choose those that interest you most, research them—and make them happen. Sounds easy, right?

Building a better future doesn't happen overnight—well, at least not in most cases. That's why it's so important that you identify the right path for you. To get there, document steps and milestones along the way. When you've decided what you'd like to accomplish, that becomes your end goal. Then work hard to get there.

The plan you develop may include smaller, short-term goals along with bigger, long-term goals. You may have chosen several things you want to aspire to, but let's focus on your main one.

My aspirations for building a brighter, successful future are:
- Achieving a college education that affords me the financial stability to provide for my son and me
- Majoring in a field that interests me, and one that would provide opportunities for growth and advancement
- Setting attainable goals, both short- and long-term, and working diligently to achieve them
- Making changes and sacrifices along the way

In the next exercises, you'll:
- Identify your end goal
- Identify your aspirations
- Build a plan that gets you there
- Note the sacrifices and lifestyle changes you'll make to achieve your goals
- Create short-term and long-term goals

Let's start by defining what interests you. What are your aspirations for achieving a brighter future?

1. _____

2. _____

3. _____

4. _____

5. _____

6. _____

7. _____

8. _____

9. _____

10. _____

Now that you've defined your aspirations, build a plan you'll use to achieve them.

In the next exercise, document the steps, the timeline, the resources, and the actions you'll take to reach your end goal(s). This plan will consist of small and large goals, as well as short-term and long-term goals.

It's important that your goals are attainable. After you've identified a few and achieved them, set a few more goals, and so on. **Objectives** are what you'll do to achieve your goals. **Actions** are the activities you'll perform, based on your **Objectives**.

I'll start by listing a few of my preliminary goals leading to my end goal of getting a degree in a field that will afford me opportunities to grow and advance.

GOAL: Pick a college major.	
OBJECTIVES	**ACTIONS**
1. Attend career fairs	1. Inquire of school officials for upcoming career fairs; research online for upcoming, nearby career fairs.
2. Research different career fields	2. Read books on various career fields and jobs; do research online; talk with professionals of various career fields.
3. Speak to an academic counselor	3. Schedule an appointment with the academic counselor at school or prospective college.
4. Schedule an informational interview with a career professional within my chosen field	4. Set up an informational interview with a career professional to get on-the-job experience.

GOAL: Earn Undergraduate Degree.	
OBJECTIVES	**ACTIONS**
1. Research colleges	1. Look into schools that are most suitable for me (convenient location, flexible program hours, affordable, accredited, etc.).
2. Enroll in college	2. Apply within.
3. Complete program within standard time-frame	3. Successfully pass every class and complete entire program within average time-frame.

GOAL:	Get a job with a company where I could apply my degree and advance.	
OBJECTIVES	**ACTIONS**	
1. Research companies where I could start with an entry-level position and work my way up as I complete my degree. 2. As I get closer to graduation, internally search for jobs within the company where I can apply my degree. 3. After completion of my degree, apply for job internally.	1. Search for entry-level positions that would provide financial stability while I complete my degree, and that would provide advancement opportunities within my field of study. 2. Start doing internal research on open jobs within my field of study (e.g., jobs within the Information Technology department, IT) as it gets closer to graduation time. 3. Apply for internal jobs within my field of study (e.g., IT Department).	

GOAL:	No more children out of wedlock and while on my journey to a better future.	
OBJECTIVES	**ACTIONS**	
1. Take necessary precaution to prevent having any more children.	1. Avoid situations that could jeopardize completing my goals or complicate them.	

In this table, define your preliminary goals for achieving your end goal, as I did above.

GOAL:	
OBJECTIVES	ACTIONS

GOAL:	
OBJECTIVES	ACTIONS

GOAL:	
OBJECTIVES	ACTIONS

GOAL:	
OBJECTIVES	ACTIONS

Please note: *Additional space to continue this exercise can be found in Appendix D.*

SECTION 4.2

Changes For The Better

Sometimes we make adjustments that support our greater purpose. While working toward your goal for a bright, successful future, you may need to alter your lifestyle to achieve the results you desire. The changes and sacrifices won't always be easy, but look at the bigger picture and you'll know it's all worth it.

When I initially set out to achieve my goals, I failed numerous times. You see, I was trying to get different results, but I was doing the same things I had always done. I thought I could be a mom, an employee, a college student, and still do the things I'd done before without changing things up.

I failed miserably at everything I had going on. It was then that I realized I had to make serious changes if I ever planned to achieve my goals. I could no longer do what I used to do before I set goals. I altered my lifestyle so I could focus on the bigger picture. Some of the changes I made included:

- Social life: spent less time socializing
- Circle of friends: surrounded myself with like-minded people and minimized distractions
- Work hours: adjusted my work hours to accommodate my full-time college schedule
- Time with family and loved ones: sacrificed time with my son so I could finish college sooner
- Summer vacations: sacrificed summer vacations in favor of summer classes
- Relationships: put romance on hold until I finished college and got my career started

So far, you've identified your aspirations, set goals, and built a plan to achieve them. Now, identify changes and sacrifices you'll have to make, as I did above. I used my changes as examples for you to follow.

CHANGE/SACRIFICE	REASON FOR CHANGE/SACRIFICE	EXPECTED OUTCOME
Social life	To successfully meet my workload, I had to cut back on my social activities.	More time for college.
Circle of friends	To surround myself with people aspiring to achieve similar outcomes, I looked for different friends and acquaintances who were also making positive changes and achieving success.	Fewer distractions and chances to be taken off course.
Work hours	To accommodate my full-time college schedule, I cut back on my work hours.	Complete college sooner rather than later.
Time with family and loved ones	Again, to accommodate my full-time college schedule, I sacrificed precious time with my son.	Complete college sooner, so I could get back to spending quality time with my son.
Summer vacations	In favor of taking summer classes, I sacrificed taking summer vacations.	Complete college sooner rather than later.
Relationships	To ensure less distraction while working toward completing my goals, I sacrificed love and long-term committed relationships.	Successfully complete my goals on time and start my career.

It's your turn!

CHANGE/SACRIFICE	REASON FOR CHANGE/SACRIFICE	EXPECTED OUTCOME

Please note: *Additional space to continue this exercise can be found in Appendix D.*

SECTION 4.3

Getting Through Obstacles And Roadblocks

Achieving your dream requires hard work. You'll encounter roadblocks along the way. These challenges are common, but **resilience** is key to overcoming them successfully. The sooner we bounce back, the better.

Life, at times, throws us curveballs and sets us back, just when we're getting close to our goal. When this happens, don't let yourself get discouraged, and don't give up because things are harder or something happens that wasn't part of your plan. Do your very best to work through any obstacles, so you get back on track sooner.

Tips for working through roadblocks:
- Stay encouraged by surrounding yourself with like-minded people, and with people who inspire you, encourage you, push you, and support you.
- Work on one goal at a time, so you do not become overwhelmed.
- Avoid any and all activities that take you off course.
- Set an end date for your goals and keep an eye on it.
- Seek help when needed ***before*** it is too late.
- Keep faith.
- Look how far you've come.
- Don't become discouraged by how much further you have to go.
- Reward yourself—often.
- Understand that *failure is **not** an option*.
- ***Believe in yourself.***
- ***NEVER GIVE UP!***

Challenges are inevitable when you're working to fulfill your dream and life goals. You need willpower and determination as you set out on your journey. Too many people make the mistake of giving up because they've hit a roadblock or two. When or if this happens, keep thinking of your end goal and how far you've already come, then reset.

Pace yourself as you work toward your goal(s). Don't take on too much at a time, and don't get discouraged by how far you have to go. Instead, focus on starting and completing one goal at a time. Remember—life is what you make of it. You CAN achieve your dreams, one goal at a time.

NOTES

CHAPTER 5

CHOOSING THE RIGHT ROLE MODEL FOR YOU

When you choose a role model, keep in mind that they're there to inspire and motivate you to improve yourself. That person should have a clear understanding of what you need to improve, and the path you've chosen to build a better future.

Role models can also help you create plans, and sometimes they can provide you with helpful resources. So, it's important to choose the right role model(s) for you and your circumstances.

There are good role models, and there are not-so-good role models. Be sure you can distinguish between the two. Be sure to steer clear of the not-so-good ones, as they will not have your best interests in mind, and they will not help you accomplish your goals.

An important step in choosing the best role model is to identify the qualities you are looking for. Those qualities may include, but are not limited to, a person's:

- Character
- Morals and values
- Credentials
- Experiences similar to yours, or someone who can relate to you in some way
- Connections and affiliations to valuable resources
- People skills
- Passion and the ability to inspire and help others

Be sure to understand that your role model's purpose is **NOT** to do your job for you. They're merely there to guide you, give you advice, and help you seek opportunities. Ultimately, **WE** have to put in the work to make our dreams a reality.

SECTION 5.1

Identifying The Right Role Model For Me

The qualities and expectations that I require of a role model will likely differ from those you require. Before choosing a role model, identify what your expectations are. This will help you improve the chances that you'll find one who is the best fit for you and who will make a positive difference for you on your journey.

In this exercise, compile a list of qualities you want a role model to have. Align the qualities with your plan and vision for your future. You may want to consider how accessible the person is, their demographics, and their education or career background. I'll start off by listing qualities I want in a role model.

THE QUALITIES I AM LOOKING FOR IN A ROLE MODEL ARE:
✓ Good personality
✓ Optimistic
✓ Ability to inspire others
✓ College-educated
✓ Career-driven
✓ Trustworthy
✓ Relatable experiences
✓ Goal-oriented

It's your turn! List the qualities here that are important in the role model you choose:

THE QUALITIES I AM LOOKING FOR IN A ROLE MODEL ARE:
✓
✓
✓
✓
✓
✓
✓
✓

Please note: *Additional space to continue this exercise can be found in Appendix E.*

Another important step in choosing your role model is to **set expectations**. Doing so will help to ensure that you'll get the right level of support. It also helps the person you choose to understand how they can help you be successful in pursuing your goals. Again, my expectations may be different from yours.

In this exercise, set expectations for your ideal role model. Be sure to align them with your plan and vision for your future. You may want to consider how accessible they'll be, their demographics, and their education or career background. I'll start first and list my expectations.

MY EXPECTATIONS FOR MY IDEAL ROLE MODEL ARE:
✓ Sounding board to bounce ideas back and forth
✓ Accessible at standard times
✓ Help guide me in the right direction
✓ Not afraid to push me when needed
✓ Help in creating opportunities and connections
✓ Honest and transparent
✓ Give advice they would follow
✓ Help to make a difference

It's your turn! List your expectations here for your ideal role model:

MY EXPECTATIONS FOR MY IDEAL ROLE MODEL ARE:
✓
✓
✓
✓
✓
✓
✓
✓

Please note: *Additional space to continue this exercise can be found in Appendix E.*

You've identified the qualities and expectations for your ideal role model, so the next step is to identify what you hope to gain from this experience. What do you want to see happen? What value will it be to you? Having this information will help your role model understand what they need to do to effectively help you pursue your goals.

💡 In these spaces, state what you hope to gain from your role model, and why each is important.

1. _____
   _____
   _____
   _____
   _____

2. _____
   _____
   _____
   _____
   _____

3. _____
   _____
   _____
   _____
   _____

4. _____
   _____
   _____
   _____
   _____

5. _____
   _____
   _____
   _____

6. _____
   _____
   _____
   _____

SECTION 5.2

Helping You Help Me

In the section just finished, we described the type of role model and support we're looking for.

In this section, we'll discuss how you'll do **your** part to help your role model be successful in helping you.

In my book, *Life In Its Rawest Form*, I talk about how we are responsible for doing the work:

"A role model isn't a book of answers. They're merely an avenue for guidance, advice, and opportunities. While you can share your goals and aspirations with your role model and get support and encouragement, we still have to put in the work ourselves. It's up to us to use these opportunities as stepping-stones, but we have to take action on our own."

Understanding the statement above is the most crucial component in benefiting from having a role model. **It's the be-all and end-all.** We must know and understand our role in this process, and we must be willing to put in the work to make it successful.

Role models don't have all of the answers, so please don't go into this with the false idea that they do. Be prepared to do the majority of the work and take responsibility for your commitments.

Now, create a plan for how you'll support your role model's efforts to guide and mentor you. Describe how you'll hold up your end of the bargain and maximize their time and support. List ways you can help your role model successfully support you.

EXAMPLE:

	HOW I CAN HELP YOU HELP ME
1.	I'll take the process seriously.
2.	I'll have an open mind.
3.	I'll follow through on my commitments.
4.	I'll try my hardest.
5.	I'll never give up.
6.	I'll give it my best.
7.	I'll be open and honest.
8.	I'll stay optimistic.
9.	I won't be afraid to try new things.
10.	I'll always communicate.

Your turn:

	HOW I CAN HELP YOU HELP ME
1.	
2.	
3.	
4.	
5.	
6.	
7.	
8.	
9.	
10.	

Please note: *Additional space to continue this exercise can be found in Appendix E.*

The previous information and exercises will steer you in the right direction in finding the best role model for you. Use this resource to guide you in seeking and maintaining a relationship with the person you choose. It will also help you identify the role models you should ***never*** seek out, as they may not be the ideal candidates for what you are looking for.

SECTION 5.3

Choose Your Role Model Wisely

As with anything else in life, the good comes with the bad. There are people who would make a great role model, and others who would never make a good role model for you—**_know the difference! Steer clear of the bad ones._** They may try to influence you negatively. If someone does not have your best interests in mind, never consider that person to be your role model, and never look to him or her for inspiration *of any kind!*

To help you avoid choosing the wrong person, know the qualities usually not possessed by a good role model. Earlier in this chapter, we focused on choosing positive and inspirational people. So now, we will focus on the opposite qualities.

Weeding out the good from the bad:

CHARACTERISTICS OF A GOOD ROLE MODEL	CHARACTERISTICS OF A BAD ROLE MODEL
<ul><li>Lives by what they teach</li><li>Law-abiding citizen and Good Samaritan in their community</li><li>Encourages and supports you</li><li>Holds an optimistic view of life</li><li>Demonstrates knowledge and understanding</li><li>Is successful and accomplished</li><li>Has high morals and values</li><li>Is respectful</li><li>Performs random acts of kindness</li></ul>	<ul><li>Does not live by what they teach</li><li>Is not law-abiding and does not help others</li><li>Discourages you and does not support you</li><li>Holds a negative view of life</li><li>Lacks common knowledge and understanding</li><li>Is unaccomplished and unsuccessful</li><li>Has poor morals and values</li><li>Is disrespectful</li><li>Does not believe in doing nice things for others</li></ul>

The table above includes just a few qualities you should avoid when choosing your role model. Also, rely on your better judgment—your gut instinct. If the bad outweighs the good, this is not the right person for you.

Section 5.4

Where To Find The Right Role Model For You

Finding the right role model isn't always quick and easy. It takes time, patience, and being open-minded. You'll want to make this process as simple as possible. The more complicated it becomes, the less chance of finding the best person.

There are many ways you can go about finding the right fit, so we'll look at a few now.

A good place to begin your search is among the people you are around on a regular basis. These people may be:

- A person you work with who has been where you are and where you're trying to go; typically this person will be someone in a higher position
- A person from your church
- A person at your school
- A friend or family member
- A community leader or activist
- A person from an organization or support group that specializes in helping people improve or advance themselves
- Someone you ask via referral for a recommendation
- A person from your social media connections and affiliations

The suggestions above are just a few ideas to get you thinking. You have a slew of avenues you can pursue in search of a role model. You'll get the best results if you methodically plan this out and take it seriously.

Section 5.5

You Can Be A Role Model, Too

Now that you've learned how, what, and what NOT to look for in a role model, you have what it takes to become a role model for someone else. Others, just like you, need someone positive to help guide and mentor them on their own journey to becoming a better person. That someone can be you! "Pay it forward." Just as someone helped you, you can help someone else. Consider being a role model as you set out on your journey to become the best person you can be.

> This exercise will show you how to be a role model for someone in need: 1) Give a brief synopsis of yourself, and 2) talk about why you would be a good role model. I'll start things off by giving a brief overview of myself and what I can offer someone as their role model.

Who Am I

My name is Qiana Hicks. I'm a mother, a college graduate, a career professional, and an author. I was born in Gary, Indiana, and raised in a single-parent home, for the most part. My parents were drug and alcohol addicts, and my father spent most of my youth in prison. I grew up living with an older brother and a younger sister.

My childhood life can be categorized as disadvantaged. Due to my mother's substance abuse problems, my biological father's absence, and my stepfather's alcohol and drug addictions, my siblings and I lived through tumultuous growing-up years. We suffered from many forms of abuse, neglect, and poverty. We were left to raise ourselves, for the most part. My family went through transition several times, where we were forced to live apart, while my mother underwent rehabilitation and incarceration. At age 15, I became an adolescent parent. I worked tirelessly to overcome the challenges of my past and position myself to face the obstacles of my future.

I finished high school on time, then enrolled in college immediately after graduation. I raised my son, and, at times, my sister, while pursuing a college degree and building a career. I later obtained a graduate degree.

I refused to allow my past to determine who and what I would become. I learned to use my past experiences as opportunities and lessons for my future. My past has made me wiser and stronger, and I hope that it will do the same for you.

Reasons Why I Would Make a Good Role Model

No one in this world is perfect. We're all unique and have different experiences, and those are the things that set us apart. But it's what we have done different to improve our future that is so important. Our experiences are opportunities to learn from and create a better future for ourselves. This is what I did so as not to repeat the sins of my past. It's been the best form of motivation, inspiration, and therapy I could have hoped for. My past is why I was able to share my life story with you (the good and the bad), hoping that it would inspire you to be better at living yours.

The reason I would make a good role model is because I have walked the walk and talked the talk. I know, firsthand, what it feels like to make something out of nothing. I know, firsthand, what it feels like to have very little hope for a better life. I believe my experiences and the wisdom I've gained from those experiences can be of help to someone else. I would commit to providing sound advice to the person I mentor, and help that person in any way I can to overcome challenges similar to mine. Coming from a single parent, disadvantaged household, I can relate to others who live in those conditions. I can also relate to growing up in an impoverished environment, where resources are scarce. All the while, I dreamed of one day having a better life. I became a mother at an early age, and most people had already counted me out as never becoming a contributing member of society. If my past experiences and how I applied them to making a better life for my son and me can inspire and motivate you, I believe I would be a good role model for you.

Now it's your turn!

Who are you?

Why would you be a good role model to others?

Please note: *Additional space to continue this exercise can be found in Appendix E.*

NOTES

CHAPTER 6

LEAVING THE PAST IN THE PAST

Harboring pain can go unnoticed for sometime. You may not realize right away that you're harboring pain from past wounds, until, that is, they begin to affect you in some way. We may trick ourselves into believing that, by ignoring the pain, it will go away without our having to do anything to fix it. We block out the pain, or pretend it never happened.

When we don't deal with our issues, they linger and prolong our suffering. Eventually, they impact our present lives in ways like:

- Our relationships
- How we interact with others
- Our job
- How we deal with situations similar to those from our past
- Our future

SECTION 6.1

Suffering May Occur In Many Forms

Trauma affects us in numerous ways, which we all deal with differently. For instance, we may easily become defensive, or more sensitive and emotional. When we're confronted about our behavior, we tend to deny it, or believe it's not happening. It's much easier not to deal with it, leaving room for the pain to linger and grow within us.

Learning how to cope with past trauma or pain is never easy—but ***it is necessary*** for our well-being. One of the most effective methods is also the simplest: just recognize that the pain or trauma exists. Effective, simple, and the first step in healing ourselves and getting resolution.

In my book, *Life In Its Rawest Form*, I talk about painful situations that have been difficult for me. They festered for quite some time, impacting various areas of my life. For a long time, I didn't realize I was harboring and suppressing them so that I didn't have to deal with the pain. The issues became an impediment to certain parts of my life, and I finally realized I needed help to address them.

In this exercise, reflect on and identify any past pain or trauma that impacts you in an unhealthy way. List painful or traumatic experiences that continue to challenge you. Also, describe the effect each experience has had on your life (e.g., anger, frustration, sadness, fear, abandonment, and so on). Feel free to include additional details as a way to heal and seek resolution. I'll go first, then it's your turn.

PAST EXPERIENCE/TRAUMA	EFFECT
I rarely received love and affection from my parents, mostly because of their drug and alcohol addictions and their childhood experiences.	I used my relationships to compensate for the love and affection I long to get from my parents.
While living in foster care and group homes, isolating myself from others became my safe haven.	Growing up, I was always uncomfortable in social settings or in groups of people.
In previous years, not fighting back to protect myself from predators.	In recent years, I've become overly defensive and, at times, I feel I'm being violated.
Growing up in an impoverished household with alcohol and drug abuse.	I'm overcome with sadness and grief whenever I see circumstances like mine. It also brings back painful memories each time.
Constant letdowns, disappointments, and my parents' unreliability.	It's difficult for me to rely upon others, because I dread being let down.

Your turn!

PAST EXPERIENCE/TRAUMA	EFFECT

Please note: *Additional space to continue this exercise can be found in Appendix F.*

Hopefully, the exercise above has made you aware of past experiences you may be harboring and that affect your life today. This is the first step in dealing with them and opening yourself for healing to occur.

SECTION 6.2

Learning To Cope With Your Past

Sometimes, coping with our unfortunate circumstances is difficult if it seems there is no cure or resolution for overcoming them. It may seem impossible to ever reach a point when the memories aren't as painful. Life seems better when you can forget about the past, or pretend it never existed. That way, you escape from a dark place to a happier, less stressful one.

That is, until the past resurfaces and hinders us from fully recovering. I can attest to this. On several occasions, just when I thought I had overcome some of my past issues, they found a way to creep back in. After repeated occurrences, I realized I hadn't learned to cope with them.

Learning to cope with trauma and painful experiences is challenging, to say the least. No one wants to face these things ever again. We would much rather make them disappear by pretending they never happened. Unfortunately, suppression won't fix the problem or allow you to heal. As difficult as it may sound, ***healing starts with facing our past issues*** and learning how to live with them so they no longer negatively affect us. There is no science to this, and what works for some may not work for others. The key is to find what works best for you.

Tips that may help you cope with trauma or painful experiences:
- Recognize they exist
- Seek clarity and understand how the trauma or pain occurred
- Accept the things you cannot change, or things that are out of your control
- Confront or address the source of your pain
- Focus on the present and the future and less on the past
- Talk to someone (family, friend, professional)
- Help others prevent the same thing from happening to them
- Look for ways to turn the negative into a positive

The next exercise will teach you various methods to cope with the experiences you described in the previous exercise. The exercise will help you identify coping mechanisms that will help you live with past experiences and trauma, while controlling how they affect you. I went first so you can use my exercise as an example when it's your turn.

PAST EXPERIENCE/ TRAUMA	EFFECT	COPING MECHANISM
I rarely received love and affection from my parents, mostly because of their drug and alcohol addictions and their childhood experiences.	I used my relationships to compensate for the love and affection I long to get from my parents.	I became content with the understanding that loving thyself is the greatest love of all. Any additional love I receive from others is a bonus.
While living in foster care and group homes, isolating myself from others became my safe haven.	Growing up, I was always uncomfortable in social settings or in groups of people.	Attend more group functions. Make a conscious effort to engage more during these events. Look for volunteer opportunities at group homes for children.
In previous years, not fighting back to protect myself from predators.	In recent years, I've become overly defensive and, at times, I feel I'm being violated.	Try harder to be emotionally aware during these times, so I don't overreact because of past experiences.
Growing up in an impoverished household with alcohol and drug abuse.	I'm overcome with sadness and grief whenever I see circumstances like mine. It also brings back painful memories each time.	Seek opportunities to help make a positive difference in communities.
Constant letdowns, disappointments, and my parents' unreliability.	It's difficult for me to rely upon others, because I dread being let down.	Work hard at trusting and relying more on others. Don't be afraid to be vulnerable, and ask for help. Treat disappointments and letdowns as opportunities.

Now, it's your turn!

PAST EXPERIENCE/ TRAUMA	EFFECT	COPING MECHANISM

Please note: *Additional space to continue this exercise can be found in Appendix F.*

Being aware helps you effectively manage your emotions, and allows you to control how they affect your life. Acknowledging that an issue or pain exists can help you live with it and heal from the experience.

Another beneficial coping tip is to look for correlations linking these past experiences with the present. Have you discovered that you're still living in the past, and that the experience(s) is/are influencing the present? Being reminded of the past isn't necessarily a bad thing. Use those memories as opportunities to prevent them from reoccurring. They'll help you make better decisions going forward. We may not be able to change what happened, but we can change ***how we allow those events to live within us***.

CHAPTER 7

MANAGING YOUR EMOTIONS EFFECTIVELY

Life doesn't always happen the way we want it to happen. At times, we'll be faced with situations that are out of our control and that challenge us to find solutions.

Hardship, abusive relationships, poverty, low self-esteem, challenges at work or school, uncertainty, losing a loved one, being a victim of bullying, family crisis, and more, are all situations that trigger our deepest emotions. These emotions can have a negative impact on our daily lives and how we'll interact with others. So, **effectively managing our emotions** is very important to our health, our relationships, and our careers, just to name a few.

Having and using the right tools and resources is essential in this quest. These tools could simply be ways to cope with situations that arise. Ultimately, you will develop a regular routine for dealing with sensitive or challenging times that will render a positive outcome.

In various challenges throughout my life, I wish I'd developed a routine that allowed me to get ahead of my emotions before they snowballed into something worse. Having these tools and resources would have kept me aware of my emotions, where I could acknowledge their cause and have a positive outcome.

In my book, I talk about situations and circumstances that made me emotional. I didn't always deal with my emotions effectively. Sometimes that made matters worse, or held me back in some way.

My goal in this section is to help you become aware of your emotions, identify with them, and create opportunities to manage them effectively. Doing so will improve individual emotional situations as they occur, **and thus** improve your life overall.

Let's start off with ways to help us when we're emotional. Then we'll move on to acknowledging and identifying the cause for our emotional state. Last, we'll create ways and opportunities for managing and controlling our emotions, and we'll identify resources that can help us do so.

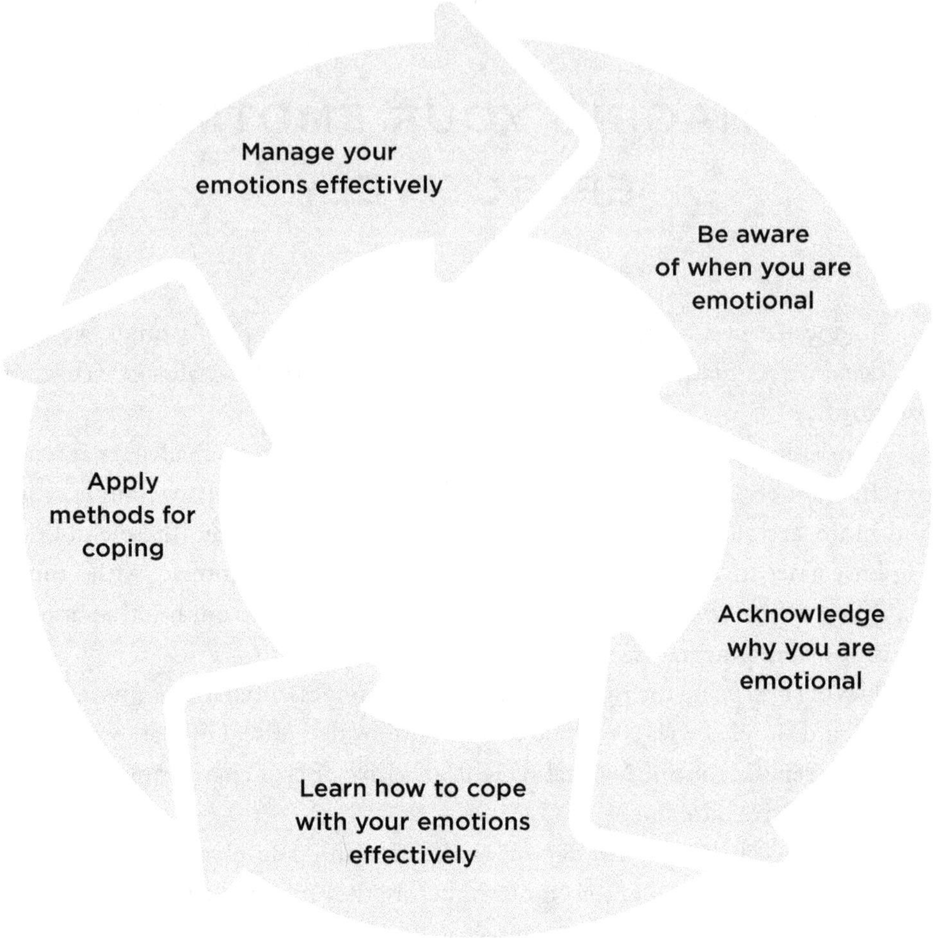

- Manage your emotions effectively
- Be aware of when you are emotional
- Acknowledge why you are emotional
- Learn how to cope with your emotions effectively
- Apply methods for coping

FIGURE 3

SECTION 7.1

Identify What Is Causing You To Become Emotional

The more we are aware of our emotions, the more successful we'll be at managing and overcoming them—possibly becoming even stronger.

The key to becoming emotionally aware is to identify and acknowledge what causes you to become emotional. You could start by:

- Reflecting on the situation or circumstances causing you to become emotional
- Talking about it with someone
- Writing about it in a journal or diary

When life throws us a curveball and takes us off course, it often comes when we least expect it. We may react in ways that are not beneficial to improving the situation or our lives. These types of reactions can become an impediment to moving forward or taking advantage of opportunities.

If we don't get ahead of our emotions by recognizing them early on, we may find that we're constantly reactive instead of proactive, thus having to spend time to correct or undo what we may not have done under normal circumstances.

In this exercise, we'll identify ways to be proactive in recognizing our emotions and effectively managing them. ***Let's aim to improve ourselves, while improving our situations.***

We'll start by reflecting on things going on right now in your life that may trigger certain emotions.

1. List any challenging situations or tragic events currently affecting you:

A. _____

B. _____

C. _____

2. Describe the type of impact each event in #1 has on your daily life:

A. _____
_____
_____

B. _____
_____
_____

C. _____
_____
_____

3. Describe how each event in #1 affects your feelings and emotions:

A. _____
_____
_____

B. _____
_____
_____

C. _____
_____
_____

SECTION 7.2

Acknowledge The Reality Of The Situation

After we identify emotional triggers, we acknowledge the nature of the situation or circumstances. These may be out of our control, leaving us to realize we don't have much influence in choosing outcomes. However, we ***can choose*** how we'll allow them to affect our lives. In this case, we ***accept*** those things we cannot change, and focus, instead, on how to cope with them daily. Acknowledging the problem helps us deal proactively with less-than-ideal situations and make the best of them.

In this section, we'll use a constructive approach that identifies opportunities to help us through these challenging times. Think outside the box. Some ideas to consider:

- Keep busy with regular chores or extracurricular activities, and focus less on the negative
- Continue to respect others, regardless of the situation or circumstance.
- Communicate your needs and avoid letting emotions build up
- Conscientiously manage your temper
- Set goals or develop a plan to deal positively with each situation
- Always keep a positive attitude

Growing up, I was faced with unfortunate situations and circumstances. Some were within my control, while others were not. I could have benefited from having a constructive approach in place to help me navigate those times, and the outcomes would have been more positive.

Living in group homes and in foster homes, I had a difficult time coping with the separation from my family. On occasion, these times affected my behavior, and how I interacted with others. I didn't know how to deal constructively with these situations. I've wondered if things would have turned out better had I taken the time to reflect on doing more positive things to get through those tough times.

We'll use the situations mentioned in the previous section to identify opportunities to help improve how we handle difficult situations, whether they're within our control or not. We'll explore options to keep us from making matters worse. Our goal is to identify several opportunities, then use them for any situation and under any circumstance.

Reflect on the brutal reality of the situation(s). What about the situation(s) can't you change and must come to terms with?

1. _____

2. _____

3. _____

List 3 to 5 things that can help you proactively deal with the reality of the things you cannot change about your situation(s):

1. _____

2. _____

3. _____

4. _____

5. _____

Describe how the situation(s) or circumstance(s) could get worse if you do not effectively deal with it:

1. _____
_____
_____

2. _____
_____
_____

3. _____
_____
_____

List 3 to 5 things that can prevent the situation(s) or circumstance(s) from getting worse:

1. _____
_____
_____

2. _____
_____
_____

3. _____
_____
_____

4. _____
_____
_____

5. _____
_____
_____

If you could improve your situation(s), what could you do better?

1. _____
_____
_____
_____

2. _____
_____
_____
_____

3. _____
_____
_____
_____

What help do you need to improve your situation(s)/circumstance(s)?

1. _____
_____
_____
_____

2. _____
_____
_____
_____

3. _____
_____
_____
_____

How can those around you (family, school officials, Family Services, etc.) help you?

1. _____

_____

_____

2. _____

_____

_____

3. _____

_____

_____

What do you hope to gain from each situation?

1. _____

_____

_____

2. _____

_____

_____

3. _____

_____

_____

Becoming emotional is inevitable. At some point, we'll all be emotional. It doesn't have to be a negative thing, as long as we are:

- Aware of when we become emotional
- Acknowledge why we're emotional
- Learn how to effectively cope with the situation

Performing the previous exercises can prevent us from making matters worse. Effectively managing our emotions isn't an easy process. It will take discipline and hard work. However, the results will be well worth it.

NOTES

APPENDIX A
CHAPTER ONE: FAMILIES BATTLING ADDICTION

1. _____
_____
_____

2. _____
_____
_____

3. _____
_____
_____

4. _____
_____
_____

5. _____
_____
_____

6. _____
_____
_____

7. _____
_____
_____

8. _____
_____

9. _____
_____

10. _____
_____

1. _____
   _____
   _____

2. _____
   _____
   _____

3. _____
   _____
   _____

4. _____
   _____
   _____

5. _____
   _____
   _____

6. _____
   _____
   _____

7. _____
   _____
   _____

8. _____
   _____
   _____

9. _____
   _____

10. _____
    _____

APPENDIX B
CHAPTER TWO: FAMILIES IN TRANSITION

YOUR EMOTIONS AND FEELINGS DURING TRANSITION
1.
2.
3.
4.
5.
6.
7.
8.
9.
10.

	EMOTIONS	PREVENTIVE MEASURES
1.		
2.		
3.		
4.		
5.		
6.		
7.		
8.		
9.		
10.		

NOTES

NOTES

NOTES

NOTES

APPENDIX C
CHAPTER THREE: TEENAGE PREGNANCY

WHAT YOU HAVE TO LOSE	WHAT YOU HAVE TO GAIN	WHO BENEFITS	WHO SUFFERS

NOTES

ADVANTAGES	DISADVANTAGES

QUALITIES I LOOK FOR IN A COMPANION
✓
✓
✓
✓
✓
✓
✓
✓
✓
✓

ADVANTAGES	DISADVANTAGES

WEEK 1	ACTIVITY:					
SUNDAY	MONDAY	TUESDAY	WEDNESDAY	THURSDAY	FRIDAY	SATURDAY
TIME:	TIME:	TIME:	TIME:	TIME:	TIME:	TIME:

WEEK 2	ACTIVITY:					
SUNDAY	MONDAY	TUESDAY	WEDNESDAY	THURSDAY	FRIDAY	SATURDAY
TIME:	TIME:	TIME:	TIME:	TIME:	TIME:	TIME:

WEEK 3	ACTIVITY:					
SUNDAY	MONDAY	TUESDAY	WEDNESDAY	THURSDAY	FRIDAY	SATURDAY
TIME:	TIME:	TIME:	TIME:	TIME:	TIME:	TIME:

WEEK 4	ACTIVITY:					
SUNDAY	MONDAY	TUESDAY	WEDNESDAY	THURSDAY	FRIDAY	SATURDAY
TIME:	TIME:	TIME:	TIME:	TIME:	TIME:	TIME:

WHAT BREAKING THE CYCLE MEANS TO ME:
1.
2.
3.
4.
5.
6.
7.
8.
9.
10.

STATISTICS SAY	I SAY	I WILL BREAK THE CYCLE BY
More than 50% of teen mothers never graduate from high school.		
Around 25% of teen moms have a second child within 24 months of their first child.		
Fewer than 2% of teen moms earn a college degree by age 30.		
Eight out of 10 teen dads don't marry the mother of their child.		

APPENDIX D
CHAPTER FOUR: SETTING GOALS AND EXECUTING THEM

GOAL:	
OBJECTIVES	**ACTIONS**

GOAL:	
OBJECTIVES	**ACTIONS**

GOAL:	
OBJECTIVES	ACTIONS

GOAL:	
OBJECTIVES	ACTIONS

GOAL:	
OBJECTIVES	ACTIONS

GOAL:	
OBJECTIVES	ACTIONS

CHANGE/SACRIFICE	REASON FOR CHANGE/SACRIFICE	EXPECTED OUTCOME

NOTES

NOTES

SAMPLE

APPENDIX E
CHAPTER FIVE: CHOOSING THE RIGHT ROLE MODEL FOR YOU

THE QUALITIES I AM LOOKING FOR IN A ROLE MODEL ARE:
✓
✓
✓
✓
✓
✓
✓
✓

MY EXPECTATIONS FOR MY IDEAL ROLE MODEL ARE:	
✓	
✓	
✓	
✓	
✓	
✓	
✓	
✓	

	HOW I CAN HELP YOU HELP ME
1.	
2.	
3.	
4.	
5.	
6.	
7.	
8.	
9.	
10.	

Now it's your turn!

Who are you?

Why would you be a good role model to others?

NOTES

SAMPLE

APPENDIX F
CHAPTER SIX: LEAVING THE PAST IN THE PAST

PAST EXPERIENCE/TRAUMA	EFFECT

NOTES

PAST EXPERIENCE/ TRAUMA	EFFECT	COPING MECHANISM

NOTES

NOTES

NOTES

APPENDIX G
CHAPTER SEVEN: MANAGING YOUR EMOTIONS EFFECTIVELY

1. _____
   _____
   _____
   _____
   _____
   _____

2. _____
   _____
   _____
   _____
   _____
   _____

3. _____
   _____
   _____
   _____
   _____
   _____

4. _____
   _____
   _____
   _____
   _____

5. _____
   _____
   _____
   _____
   _____

6. _____
_____
_____
_____
_____

7. _____
_____
_____
_____
_____

8. _____
_____
_____
_____
_____

9. _____
_____
_____
_____
_____

10. _____
_____
_____
_____
_____

11. _____
_____
_____
_____
_____

12. _____
_____
_____
_____
_____

13. _____
_____
_____
_____
_____

14. _____
_____
_____
_____
_____

15. _____
_____
_____
_____
_____

16. _____

17. _____

18. _____

www.ingramcontent.com/pod-product-compliance
Lightning Source LLC
Chambersburg PA
CBHW080412300426
44113CB00015B/2486